Emerging Democracy in Indonesia

RENEWALS 458-4574

The **Institute of Southeast Asian Studies (ISEAS)** was established as an autonomous organization in 1968. It is a regional centre dedicated to the study of socio-political, security and economic trends and developments in Southeast Asia and its wider geostrategic and economic environment.

The Institute's research programmes are the Regional Economic Studies (RES, including ASEAN and APEC), Regional Strategic and Political Studies (RSPS), and Regional Social and Cultural Studies (RSCS).

ISEAS Publications, an established academic press, has issued more than 1,000 books and journals. It is the largest scholarly publisher of research about Southeast Asia from within the region. ISEAS Publications works with many other academic and trade publishers and distributors to disseminate important research and analyses from and about Southeast Asia to the rest of the world.

Emerging Democracy in Indonesia

by

Aris Ananta

Evi Nurvidya Arifin

Leo Suryadinata

INSTITUTE OF SOUTHEAST ASIAN STUDIES
Singapore

First published in Singapore in 2005 by
Institute of Southeast Asian Studies
30 Heng Mui Keng Terrace
Pasir Panjang
Singapore 119614

E-mail: publish@iseas.edu.sg
Website: <http://bookshop.iseas.edu.sg>

The responsibility for facts and opinions in this publication rests exclusively with the authors and their interpretations do not necessarily reflect the views or the policy of the publisher or its supporters.

ISEAS Library Cataloguing-in-Publication Data

Ananta, Aris.
    Emerging democracy in Indonesia / Aris Ananta, Evi Nurvidya Arifin and
    Leo Suryadinata.
    1.   Democracy—Indonesia.
    2.   Political parties—Indonesia.
    3.   Elections—Indonesia.
    4.   Indonesia—Politics and government—1998–
    I.   Arifin, Evi Nurvidya.
    II. Suryadinata, Leo, 1941–
    III. Title
JQ776 A541   2005

ISBN 981-230-322-7 (soft cover)
ISBN 981-230-323-5 (hard cover)

Cover photo: Courtesy of Toto Santiko Budi / Jiwafoto.com

Typeset by Superskill Graphics Pte Ltd
Printed in Singapore by Oxford Graphic Printers Pte Ltd

Contents

List of Figures

List of Tables

Foreword

With the fall of Soeharto in May 1998, Indonesia entered the era of *Reformasi*. The authoritarian regime was terminated and replaced by a democratic process, as manifested in the 1999 election. Four years later, in 2004, Indonesia had a second democratic election, which was also conducted in a peaceful and orderly manner. With 24 political parties, more than 500,000 polling stations and 150 million eligible voters, the Indonesian election in 2004 was probably one of the largest single-day electoral events in human history. Indeed, it is significant that Indonesia, the world's largest Muslim country, has taken major steps towards the consolidation of democratic institutions and the notion of citizenry participation has begun to take root. Indonesia's new constitutional and electoral process and the effects that the elections may have on the future conduct of Indonesian politics and the neighboring states of ASEAN deserve careful study.

ISEAS held several seminars on various aspects of the Indonesian 2004 election. The behind-the-scene stage play and the twists and turns of the Indonesian elections were closely monitored. However, to make sense out of these developments required analysis by a team of experts who thoroughly understood the Indonesian political scene. At ISEAS, the Indonesia research team, comprising of Dr Aris Ananta, Dr Evi Nurvidya Arifin and Dr Leo Suryadinata, conducted a study on the 2004 election and examined Indonesia's continuous quest for democracy in the post-Soeharto Indonesia. The study compared the 1999 and the 2004 parliamentary elections at the national level, followed by an analysis of the elections at the provincial level. One of the major features of this book is the inclusion of both statistical information and analysis, which will help the reader better understand the political situation in the fourth most populous country in the world.

I would like to congratulate the authors for undertaking their project and publishing it at a time when Indonesian democratization is drawing world attention. A lot is at stake, both for Indonesia and the region, as that country struggles to make economic and social progress amidst the growing manifestation of the "people's will".

K. Kesavapany
Director
Institute of Southeast Asian Studies
Singapore

Preface

There is no doubt that the 2004 elections in Indonesia were both interesting and important. We at the Institute of Southeast Asian Studies (ISEAS) have followed the elections with great interest. On 6 August 2004, soon after the first round of the presidential elections, we held a seminar at ISEAS to present our preliminary findings. This book is partly based on that seminar.

We have been able to complete our work, thanks to the currently mushrooming availability of statistics on Indonesian politics in general and elections in particular.

First of all, the work of the *Komisi Pemilihan Umum* (KPU, or General Elections Commission) in producing the data has been very instrumental to our work. Without their data and their willingness to share with the public, this book would never have been written. Second, many institutes have conducted polling surveys regularly and the data they gathered have strengthened our analysis on Indonesian politics and elections, otherwise most of our explanations would have been based on "educated guesses" and some anecdotal evidence. Our particular gratitude goes to the Lembaga Penelitian, Pendidikan dan Penerangan Ekonomi dan Sosial (LP3ES, or Institute for Social and Economic Research, Education & Information), IFES (International Foundation for Election Systems), Lembaga Survey Indonesia (LSI or Indonesian Survey Institute), and NDI (National Democratic Institute for International Affairs) for providing the public with survey results which have been used in this book.

We would also like to convey our deep appreciation to Mr Kesavapany, Director of ISEAS, for his constant encouragement and Mrs Triena Ong, Managing Editor of ISEAS, for her editorial assistance.

Of course, errors and shortcomings are the responsibility of the authors.

About the Authors

Aris Ananta, Ph.D., is a Senior Research Fellow at the Institute of Southeast Asian Studies, Singapore. An economist-demographer, with special expertise on Indonesia, he has been working on Indonesian politics since the beginning of 2003.

Evi Nurvidya Arifin, Ph.D., is a Visiting Fellow at the Institute of Southeast Asian Studies, Singapore. She is a social statistician, working on inter-disciplinary research projects, especially on issues related to Indonesia.

Leo Suryadinata, Ph.D., is a Senior Research Fellow at the Institute of Southeast Asian Studies, Singapore. A political scientist, he was previously a Professor at the Department of Political Science, National University of Singapore. He has published extensively on Indonesian politics, foreign policy and ethnic Chinese.

Glossary

DPR	Dewan Perwakilan Rakyat (House of Representatives/Parliament)
DPD	Dewan Perwakilan Daerah (Regional Representatives Council)
DPRD 1	Dewan Perwakilan Rakyat Daerah 1 (Provincial House of Representatives/Provincial Parliament)
Golkar	Golongan Karya (Functional Group), also known as Partai Golkar (Golkar Party)
Golput	Golongan Putih ("White Group")
ICMI	Ikatan Cendekiawan Muslim Indonesia (Association of the Indonesian Muslim Intellectuals)
IFES	International Foundation for Election Systems
IPKI	Ikatan Pendukung Kemerdekaan Indonesia (League for the Upholding of Indonesian Independence)
KKN	Korupsi, Kolusi, Nepotisme (Corruption, Collusion, Nepotism)
Koalisi Kebangsaan	National Coalition
Koalisi Kerakyatan	People's Coalition
KPU	Komisi Pemilihan Umum (General Election Commission)
Krisna	Partai Kristen Nasional Indonesia (Indonesian Christian National Party)
LP3ES	Lembaga Penelitian, Pendidikan dan Penerangan Ekonomi dan Sosial (Institute

	for Social and Economic Research, Education and Information)
LSI	Lembaga Survey Indonesia (Indonesian Survey Institute)
Masyumi	Majelis Syuro Muslimin Indonesia (Consultative Council of Indonesian Muslims)
Merdeka-Partai	Freedom Party
MK	Mahkamah Konstitusi (Constitutional Court)
MPR	Majelis Permusyawaratan Rakyat (People's Consultative Assembly)
MURBA	Party of Masses
NDI	National Democratic Institute for International Affairs
NU	Nahdlatul Ulama (Association of Islamic Scholars)
PAN	Partai Amnat Nasional (National Mandate Party)
PARKINDO	Partai Kristen Indonesia (Indonesian Christian Party)
Partai Katolik	Catholic Party
PARTINDO	Partai Indonesia (Indonesian Party)
PBB	Partai Bulan Bintang (Crescent Star Party)
PBR	Partai Bintang Reformasi (Reformed Star Party)
PBSD	Partai Buruh Sosial Demokrat (Social Democratic Labour Party)
PD	Partai Demokrat (Democrat Party)
PDI	Partai Demokrasi Indonesia (Indonesian Democratic Party)
PDI-P	Partai Demokrasi Indonesia-Perjuangan (Indonesian Democratic Party of Struggle)
PDKB	Love the Nation Democratic Party
PDS	Partai Damai Sejahtera (Prosperous Peace Party)
Perti	Pergerakan Tarbiyah Islamiah (Islamic Educational Movement)
PK	Partai Keadilan (Justice Party)

PKB	Partai Kebangkitan Bangsa (National Awakening Party)
PKD	Democratic Catholic Party
PKI	Partai Komunis Indonesia (Indonesian Communist Party)
PKPB	Partai Karya Peduli Bangsa (Concern for the Nation Functional Party)
PKPI	Partai Keadilan dan Persatuan Indonesia (Indonesian Justice and Unity Party)
PKS	Partai Keadilan Sejahtera (Prosperous Justice Party)
PNBK	Partai Nasional Banteng Kemerdekaan (Freedom Bull National Party)
PNI	Partai Nasional Indonesia (Indonesian National Party)
PNIM	PNI Marhaenisme (Marhaenism Indonesian National Party)
PPDI	Partai Penegak Demokrasi Indonesia (Indonesian Democratic Vanguard Party)
PPNU	Partai Persatuan Nahdlatul Ummah Indonesia (Indonesian Nahdlatul Community Party)
PPP	Partai Persatuan Pembangunan (United Development Party)
PSI	Partai Sarikat Indonesia (Indonesian Unity Party)
PSII	Partai Syarikat Islam Indonesia (Indonesian Islamic Union Party)
Sekber Golkar	Sekretariat Bersama Golongan Karya (Joint Secretariat of the Functional Group)
Partai Pelopor	Pioneers' Party
Partai Patriot Pancasila	Pancasila Patriots' Party

Introduction
The Road to Democracy

Although Indonesia declared independence about sixty years ago, there have only been three free elections: the 1955 election under the parliamentary system, and the 1999 and 2004 elections under the presidential system. It has been a long journey towards democracy. The first experiment in democratic elections was in 1955 but was short-lived as it was interrupted by rebellions, the semi-authoritarian government of the Guided Democracy, and the eventual military takeover in 1966. Only after the overthrow of President Soeharto, following the economic crisis and 1998 civil unrest, did the second free election — in 1999 — take place. The third, in 2004, were unique and important as they were peacefully conducted and included the first direct presidential elections in the political history of Indonesia.

Prelude: Political Parties and Democratic Elections

Indonesian political history can be divided into at least four periods: the Liberal or Constitutional Democracy Period (1949–58), the Guided Democracy Period (1959–65), the *Pancasila* Democracy Period (also known as New Order, 1966–21 May 1998) and the *Reformasi* Period (also known as the Post-Soeharto Period, May 1998–present). It was during the first period that there was a free election during which political parties played significant roles. Fifty-two parties contested in the first general election held in 1955,[1] ten years after Indonesia declared independence in 1945. Four parties, namely the Partai Nasional Indonesia (PNI, or Indonesian Nationalist Party), Majelis Syuro Muslimin Indonesia (Masyumi, or Consultative Council of Indonesian

Muslims), Nahdlatul Ulama (NU, or Association of Islamic Scholars) and Partai Komunis Indonesia (PKI, or Indonesian Communist Party), emerged as major players, receiving 22 per cent, 20 per cent, 18 per cent and 16 per cent of the total vote respectively. These four parties were seen as representing two different political cultures: the PNI and PKI represented secularism while Masyumi and NU, Islamic culture.[2] In the era of nationalism, the former could be classified as secular nationalism while the latter as Islamic nationalism.

When Soekarno introduced his Guided Democracy during which he reduced the number of political parties from over forty to ten, a major party, Masyumi, was banned due to its involvement in the 1958 rebellions aimed at overthrowing the Soekarno government. These ten parties were the PNI, NU, PKI, Perti (Pergerakan Tarbiyah Islamiah or Islamic Educational Movement), PSII (Partai Syarikat Islam Indonesia or Indonesian Islamic Union Party), Partai Murba (Party of Masses), Parkindo (Partai Kristen Indonesia or Indonesian Christian Party), Partai Katolik (Catholic Party), Partindo (Partai Indonesia or Indonesian Party), and IPKI (Ikatan Pendukung Kemerdekaan Indonesia or League for the Upholding of Indonesian Independence). These ten parties could be roughly divided into two clusters: secular nationalist and Islamic nationalist or the *Pancasila* and Islamic parties. While the former were to establish a pluralist secular state where religion is separated from the state and there is no state religion, the latter favoured the establishment of an Islamic order or a state based on *syari'ah* law.

During Soekarno's period of Guided Democracy, these political parties, with the exception of the PKI (Indonesian Communist Party), did not play a significant role. There was no general election and real politics was played outside the parliament. There was fierce competition between the army and the PKI, and this resulted in the September 1965 coup. The PKI was crushed, Soekarno was overthrown and the military came to power represented by strongman General Soeharto.

Soeharto decided to adopt a "democratic system" by introducing controlled elections. He retained the existing parties minus the PKI and Partindo. However, since there was no party which could represent the military interests, Sekber Golkar (Joint Secretariat of the Functional Group) was transformed as Golkar (Suryadinata 1989). Sekber Golkar was established in 1964 as a fusion of various anti-communist organizations. Golkar was later transformed into the political arm of the Indonesian Armed Forces and became the electoral vehicle of

General Soeharto during the New Order, from 1966 to 1998. It also became the symbol of the Javanese secular party. Nevertheless, towards the end of Soeharto's rule, Golkar was gradually changed into a Soeharto-controlled civilian party and the leadership was transferred to many non-Javanese Himpunan Mahasiswa Islam (HMI or Islamic Students Association) leaders. Dr B.J. Habibie, who was originally from Sulawesi and was also the chairman of ICMI (Indonesian Islamic Intellectual Association), became the chairman of Golkar.

In the 1971 elections, Golkar contested and won a single majority victory, winning 62.8 per cent of the votes or 236 out of 360 seats in the parliament, large enough to control the legislature. The old parties were left behind. For example, the PNI, the winning party in the 1955 election, only managed to secure 6.9 per cent of the votes. The New Order regime gave economic development top priority, but suppressed political development. To further consolidate his power, Soeharto in 1973 restructured the nine old parties and fused them into two "new" parties: the Partai Demokrasi Indonesia (PDI) and Partai Persatuan Pembangunan (PPP). The PDI comprised the PNI, Parkindo, Partai Katolik, Partai Murba and IPKI, while the PPP consisted of the NU, Parmusi (a new Islamic party that had emerged prior to the 1971 election), Perti, and PSII. In 1984 these two parties and Golkar were required to embrace *Pancasila* as their only ideology. However, only Golkar and the PDI-P were perceived by voters as secular parties, while the PPP was seen as an Islamic party.

It was under the authoritarian rule that Soeharto conducted his controlled elections, six times in total (1971, 1977, 1982, 1987, 1992 and 1997), with only three political parties competing. The government had controlled the electorate tightly and put pressure on them to vote for Golkar (Suryadinata 2002). It was not surprising, therefore, that Golkar won a landslide victory in each of these elections, while the PPP and the PDI failed to challenge the government electoral machine. However, the performance of the PPP was still better than the PDI, which was relegated to an insignificant position.

The May 1997 election was the last one under the New Order, when Golkar's victory was at the peak of its political history, winning 74.5 per cent of the votes, while the PPP gained only 22.5 per cent, and the PDI 11.9 per cent.

The twenty-first of May 1998 was the day that marked the end of the New Order. After a series of demonstrations and riots, Soeharto agreed to surrender his power to the vice president, Dr B.J. Habibie.

Habibie was supposed to rule Indonesia for the rest of the Soeharto term (1998–2003). However, many considered him a Soeharto man and hence would not meet the aspirations of the Indonesians. He was a transitional president. The new authority, knowing that it was difficult to continue the authoritarian rule, quickly loosened up the control. There was a call for a more democratic political system and Habibie faced a new situation which needed him to be more responsive especially towards the opposition groups. Habibie's administration immediately began to liberalize laws on elections and political parties and prepared for a new election, scheduled for 1999. Thus, the process of developing a new framework for democratic elections had begun.

The government succeeded in preparing various laws to conduct a relatively free and fair election, the first democratic election in post-authoritarian rule, due in June 1999. The restriction to only three political parties during the New Order was removed under Habibie. Responding to this new-found freedom, Indonesians started to organize themselves and formed various political parties. The number of political parties exploded and was reported to reach 145 parties, ranging from major parties to small parties. Some of them did not survive in the selection process to contest in the election. Finally, forty-eight parties contested in the 1999 election, which included eighteen parties with Islamic ideology.

Five years later, Indonesians experienced more democratic elections. A major step forward was taken. Indonesians were able to elect directly their representatives and also their president. To establish more democratic elections, Indonesians had reformed and set up a complicated system and a lengthy political process under Law no. 31/2002 (Political Parties), Law no. 12/2003 (General and Regional Elections) and Law no. 23/2003 (Presidential Election).

New Electoral System: The 2004 Elections

The year 2004 was one full of politics which had offered hope and encouragement towards a democratic society. Indonesians had debated, changed and implemented every fundamental aspect of the state which resulted in, for example, an amended constitution, parliament and election system. Indeed, the 2004 elections were not a simple process.

With the continued euphoria of having the freedom to form political parties after the fall of the then President Soeharto in 1998, there was a burgeoning of many political parties. Initially, about 150 political parties were registered at the Ministry of Justice and Human

Rights for the 2004 elections, but only fifty parties passed the initial test. After going through scrutiny by the Komisi Pemilihan Umum (KPU or General Elections Commission), only twenty-four political parties (half of the parties in the 1999 election) eventually fulfilled the legal requirements to contest in 2004. Most of about 150 million eligible voters — which was about 20 per cent more than in 1999, stretched across 14,000 islands and three time zones, and needed around 500,000 to 600,000 voting stations — went into 2,025 electoral districts. To have a smooth implementation, the election process relied heavily upon 3.5 million staff and 1 million security officers. Nearly a billion ballot papers were needed and had to reach the numerous islands in the archipelago. Therefore, logistics was one of many challenges faced by the new election system.

When compared with previous elections, the 2004 elections had more differences than similarities. For the first time, voters faced three phases of elections: the parliamentary (legislative) election on 5 April, and the presidential elections on 5 July and 20 September 2004. The parliamentary election, also for the first time, elected members of the DPR (House of Representatives/Parliament), the DPD (regional representatives council), and members of the DPRDs (provincial/district parliaments).

Overall, up to 475,000 candidates were nominated by the twenty-four contesting political parties. The DPD attracted more than 1,200 candidates. To choose the DPD candidates, each voter had to choose one candidate only. For the DPR, 7,756 candidates passed the verification process to compete for the 550 seats. A proportional system with an open list was used for the parliamentary election. With this new system, voters could, for the first time, vote for a candidate as well as a political party which nominated the chosen candidate.

Both the DPR and DPD constitute the new MPR (national assembly). The assembly had 678 members, consisting of 550 elected DPR members representing political parties and 128 DPD members representing the regional communities (four members for each of the 32 provinces). The DPR is still the most powerful legislative body. It is more democratic in the sense that it comprises only elected members. In the 1999 election, thirty-eight seats were reserved for the military but these seats were abolished in the 2004 parliament.

The DPD is a new institution. The members were also elected in their own individual capacity, not based on their party affiliation. Unlike Utusan Daerah (regional representatives) who were in the past either selected by political parties or the government, the representatives in the DPD were directly elected by the voters. Nevertheless, unlike DPR members, these DPD members do not have the right to propose legislative bills. This system serves as a senate-type institution in the Indonesian parliamentary system.

The outcome of the results of the first phase held on 5 April 2004 had a major impact on the presidential poll held on 5 July 2004. This was Indonesia's first direct presidential elections. Though the president was directly elected by Indonesian voters, political parties still played important roles as the direct presidential election law did not allow an independent candidate to contest, unless he or she was nominated by a political party that had obtained at least 3 per cent of the DPR seats or 5 per cent of the total vote. Nevertheless, a party that did not meet this condition could combine forces with other parties to nominate their candidates. Political parties were also allowed to nominate a person who was not originally a party member. This would enable some well-known NGO leaders to contest the seat and broaden the slate of candidates. The July election was often referred to as the first round of the presidential elections to elect the new president. Because no pair of presidential and vice presidential candidates won a single majority (50 per cent plus 1), the second round was unavoidable, and was conducted on 20 September 2004.

The 2004 elections had attracted many observers, both national and international. They were unique because they had been subjected to many polling surveys. Highly accurate national quick counts of actual results from polling stations had been conducted by the LP3ES and within one or two days after the elections, people could have clear ideas of who would win and by what percentages. The accessibility and use of these statistics have influenced laymen as well as politicians to better understand Indonesian politics. The mushrooming of statistics on elections (and politics) can also be seen as another indicator of a rising democracy in Indonesia. Some of those who did not do well in the elections had complained that the results of the surveys should not have been published; it was argued that such publications would only help to boost those who were leading in popularity. Even so, these statistics did indeed help raise the awareness and knowledge of both laymen and politicians on the real situation of the politics in general and the elections in particular — rather than relying on speculation.[3]

Focusing on the 2004 elections, this book examines the process of democratization in Indonesia, a developing country with the Muslim population as the majority, through a massive election process conducted throughout most of the year of 2004. A distinguishing feature of this book is the use of the statistics to contribute to a better understanding of electoral behaviour in Indonesia.[4] The book, and particularly the utilization of the statistics, is expected to provide a much needed contribution to the literature on Indonesia's democratic development.

Chapter 1 discusses democracy at work in the post-authoritarian Soeharto regime, focusing on the democratic 2004 parliamentary election at the national level. It starts with an examination of the winning parties in both the 1999 and 2004 parliamentary elections. It is then followed by discussions on the emergence of new parties and splits within major parties, closing with the new, democratically elected, DPR and MPR.

Furthermore, democracy has been going beyond the national level. The laws on regional autonomy implemented since 2001 have brought the regions within Indonesia into prominence. Therefore Chapter 2 analyses the regional variations of the 2004 parliamentary election results. It discusses the performance of the six surviving parties, two emerging medium parties, and four small parties at the provincial level.

The parliamentary election was followed by the presidential elections. Chapter 3 examines the individual popularity of potential candidates for the first round of the presidential elections according to the polling surveys conducted after December 2003. Descriptions of the five official pairs of presidential-vice presidential candidates are presented, as is the popularity of the "losing" and "winning" pairs of the official candidates. It discusses the apparent "inconsistency" between the votes gained by the parties and those obtained by their nominated candidates. A case in point is the meteoric rise of Yudhoyono and his running mate, Kalla.

The emergence of the Yudhoyono–Kalla team is discussed in Chapter 4. This chapter examines the choice between "the proven track records" (referring to the Megawati–Hasyim camp) and "change" (the Yudhoyono–Kalla camp), and the popularity ratings of the candidates in the two months before the second round. A comparison of the performance of the finalists in the first and second rounds at the national and provincial levels reveals in which provinces each of the two pairs (Yudhoyono–Kalla and Megawati–Hasyim) enjoyed their victories. There is an analysis of the poor performance of the National Coalition in boosting the support for Megawati–Hasyim. The background characteristics of the supporters — such as age, education, ethnicity and religion — together with the criteria the voters would use to choose their president, are discussed at the end of this chapter.

The last chapter concludes the book by re-examining the peaceful transition toward democracy that Indonesia has just experienced. It first discusses the significance of the 2004 elections in Indonesia's political system, especially the party system. It then describes President Yudhoyono and the formation of the new cabinet. Finally, it ends with a note on the continuing quest for democracy.

Notes

1. Of 52 competing parties, 28 parties (or about 54 per cent of the competing parties) managed to get one or more seats of 257 elected seats in the parliament. In addition to these seats, there were a number of appointed seats allocated for Irian Jaya, which did not participate in the election due to the occupation of the Dutch, and also for non-indigenous ethnic minorities. The 1955 election consisted of 16 electoral districts, namely, North Sumatra, Central Sumatra, South Sumatra, Greater Jakarta, West Java, Central Java, East Java, East Nusa Tenggara, West Nusa Tenggara, West Kalimantan, South Kalimantan, East Kalimantan, North Sulawesi, South Sulawesi, Maluku, and Irian Jaya (Suryadinata 2002). The turnout was high with 91.5 per cent of the registered voters, or about 39 million voters.

2. For a discussion of the political parties and their political cultures, see Suryadinata (2002), chapter 1.

3. Some observers, analysts, and politicians may be sceptical of the quality of these statistics. They may be right, but the use of these statistics are still much better than evaluation based on guesswork. More importantly, most statistics used in this book were produced by reliable institutions. The characteristics of the respondents in their samples were close to those in the Indonesian population census.

4. This book, and the use of statistics as its distinguishing feature, is actually a continuation of what the authors did in *Indonesian Electoral Behaviour. A Statistical Perspective* (Singapore: Institute of Southeast Asian Studies, 2004), which examines the 1999 election in relation to some social and economic conditions.

1

Democracy at Work
The 2004 Parliamentary Elections

There was no democracy during the Soeharto era as Indonesia was under an authoritarian rule and the six general elections during the New Order were conducted undemocratically. The dawn of democracy only emerged after the fall of the then President Soeharto when genuine political parties were formed and free and fair elections were held. The 1999 election was the first such elections, followed by the 2004 elections. The latter was even more democratic as the president was directly elected by the people. Along with the 1999 election, the 2004 parliamentary election has paved the way towards Indonesia's emerging democracy, the major theme of this book.

This chapter examines Indonesia's democracy by focusing on the 2004 parliamentary election. As it is the second democratic election after the fall of Soeharto in 1998, the chapter also briefly discusses the 1999 election. It studies the emergence of new parties, split within major parties, and the new DPR and MPR with its political dynamics.

The 1999 Election and Winning Parties[1]

In 1998, Indonesians began to enjoy political freedom and form new political parties — an important step towards democracy. The earlier restrictions on forming political parties were abolished and interference by the government into the parties' internal affairs was not allowed. There were 148 registered parties, but only forty-eight qualified to contest the election. Unlike before, the post-Soeharto elections allowed an unlimited number of parties of different ideologies (including Islam) to contest the elections provided that they fulfilled the requirement of having branches in at least half of the districts, in each of nine out of the twenty-seven provinces in Indonesia. Of the forty-eight parties, eighteen or more than one third were Islamic parties, and the rest were *Pancasila* parties. As in 1955, the 1999 election was also based on the parliamentary system — that the Indonesian voters chose their representatives in the parliament and the parliament then chose the president and vice president.

The results of the 1999 election were significant in that there was no more dominant party, thus ending the era of one-party (Golkar) dominance. Political power became fragmented. The largest party — the PDI-P — of Megawati won the first place, followed by Golkar and other major and medium parties as seen in Figure 1.1.

FIGURE 1.1
Results of the 1999 Election: Indonesia

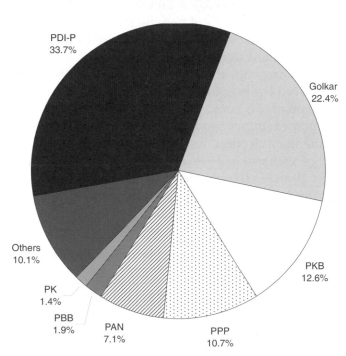

Source: Calculated from Table 1.1.

The Partai Demokrasi Indonesia-Perjuangan (PDI-P) was originally called the Partai Demokrasi Indonesia (PDI) during the New Order period. It was the smallest party during the New Order and had performed poorly during the controlled elections. However, when Megawati Soekarnoputri, the eldest daughter of the then President Soekarno, joined the party, it soon began to be noticed by the authorities. In 1987, she was elected chairperson of the PDI Jakarta branch. In December 1993 during the Extraordinary Meeting in Surabaya, she was elected General Chairperson of the PDI for the term of 1993–98. However, in 1996, before her term ended, the Soeharto regime was worried about her rising popularity and it sponsored Soerjadi, the former chairman of the PDI, to engineer a "coup", seizing the chairpersonship from Megawati. It was only after the fall of Soeharto (in May 1998) that Megawati recaptured the party leadership. Nevertheless, the rival PDI was still in existence. On 14 February 1999, Megawati proclaimed the foundation of the Partai Demokrasi Indonesia Perjuangan or shortened as the PDI-P, and became its first chairperson.

Perceived as less Islamic and more Javanese, the underdog PDI-P participated in the 1999 election and won 33.7 per cent of the total vote, occupying the first place. However, in the presidential election in the MPR, Megawati was defeated by Abdurrahman Wahid (Gus Dur) of a smaller party, the PKB. Megawati settled for the vice-presidency of the Republic of Indonesia. Only after the sudden removal of the then President Gus Dur by the MPR, did she fill the vacancy of the presidential post in July 2001. She was required to hold the mandate until the presidential term ended in 2004. Megawati was then the president of Indonesia though she had little experience in politics. She had only been active in the Gerakan Mahasiswa Nasional Indonesia (GMNI, or Indonesian National Student Movement) during her student days. She briefly studied in the Department of Agriculture at the Padjajaran University (1965–67) and the Department of Psychology at the University of Indonesia (1971–72).

The second largest party in the 1999 election, Golkar won 22.4 per cent of the total vote. Akbar Tanjung, a Batak, who was the chairman of the HMI and served as minister under Soeharto, became the leader of the party. Like the PDI-P, Golkar also used *Pancasila* as the ideology of the party; but, unlike the PDI-P, Golkar's image was that of being non-Javanese and being a party with Islamic leanings.

The third largest party (12.7 per cent) was the Partai Kebangkitan Bangsa (PKB, or National Awakening Party), a political organization with the Nahdlatul Ulama (NU), the largest Islamic social organization in Indonesia, as the main constituent. The party was only established after the fall of Soeharto, and headed by Matori Abdul Djalil, but the man behind it was actually Gus Dur, former general chairman of the NU. The NU in the 1950s was against *Pancasila*, but the leadership of Gus Dur changed its political stand and accepted *Pancasila* as the Indonesian ideology. He was even quoted as saying that *Pancasila* was the last form of Indonesian ideology. Not surprisingly, the PKB embraced *Pancasila* as the party ideological base. The PKB is basically an East Java-based party and the supporters are mainly Javanese.

The fourth largest party (10.7 per cent) was the Partai Persatuan Pembangunan (PPP, or United Development Party), a loyal opposition party during the New Order but, like Golkar, it managed to survive after the fall of Soeharto. Unlike the PKB, the PPP declared it was an Islamic party, no longer based on *Pancasila*; also unlike the PKB, the PPP support came more from the non-Javanese Muslims. The chairman of the PPP is Hamzah Haz, a Kalimantan-born Muslim who is a member of the NU. He was a journalist and a lecturer of economics at Tanjungpura University in Pontianak, West Kalimantan. He started his political life by joining the parliament in the province of West Kalimantan in 1971. He served as minister for investment in the Habibie cabinet and co-ordinating minister for social welfare for a hundred days during Gus Dur's administration. In 2001 he was elected as vice president in Megawati's government.

The fifth largest party (7.0 per cent) was Partai Amanat Nasional (PAN, or National Mandate Party), established by Dr Amien Rais, once the chairperson of the Muhammadiyah, the second largest Indonesian Islamic social organization. Muhammadiyah was part of the Masyumi party, which, in the 1950s, was against *Pancasila* as the political ideology of Indonesia. Nevertheless, the PAN of Amien Rais declared it was a party based on *Pancasila* rather than Islam, though the Muhammadiyah was its major constituent. PAN was interested in getting the support of both Muslims and non-Muslims. Amien was educated in Muhammadiyah schools until he was eighteen. He later went to the Gadjah Mada University before going overseas for higher studies. He earned an M.A. degree in Sociology from the University of Notre Dame, with a thesis on Egypt's foreign policy. He obtained his Ph.D. in political science from the University of Chicago, with a dissertation on Egypt's Islamic Movement. After returning to Indonesia he was involved in the establishment of the Association of the Indonesian Muslim Intellectuals (ICMI), headed by Dr B.J. Habibie, and was the chairman of the Experts Council of ICMI during the 1999 election. Because of his Islamic leaning,

Amien's party support appears to have come from Muslims rather than non-Muslims. Amien is a professor at the Gadjah Mada University and also known as a reform leader (*tokoh reformasi*). He was a major figure in mobilizing the masses to force Soeharto to step down during the last days of the New Order. As a result of the 1999 election, he was elected and served as the chairman of the MPR in 1999–2004.

The sixth largest party (1.9 per cent), the Partai Bulan Bintang (PBB, or Crescent Star Party), was established after the fall of Soeharto. It was led by Dr Yusril Ihza Mahendra, a Bangka-born Malay who is a graduate from the Law School of the University of Indonesia. He obtained a Ph.D. from the Universiti Sains in Penang, Malaysia. Like Amien, Yusril was also an activist of ICMI and was elected a chairperson of the Jakarta branch. His PBB is based on Islam.

Another new party (established in July 1998) which was also based on Islam was Partai Keadilan (PK, or Justice Party). It was a *dakwah* party, or an Islamic party which intended to spread the teaching of Islam. It won 1.4 per cent of the total votes in the 1999 election. The leader of this party was Dr Ir Nur Mahmud Ismail, a graduate from the Agricultural Institute in Bogor. He later went to Texas to specialize in food and science technology and received both an M.Sc. and Ph.D. degree.[2] He was not known in the political arena. However, the PK was active on college campuses in the post-Soeharto years and won many Muslim student followers. Its support came from the educated Islamic community not only in Java but also in the outer islands. It competed with other Islamic parties but, because of its limited circle, it was unable to secure many votes.

These seven parties were considered to be either major or medium parties after the 1999 election. However, none of these parties was able to form a government independently as no party was able to gain more than 50 per cent of the vote (see Table 1.1). Of interest is the proportion of votes between the *Pancasila* parties and the Islamic parties. If the PKB and PAN are excluded from the category of Islamic parties, the combined votes of Islamic parties in 1999 was only 17.7 per cent;[3] but if the PKB and PAN are considered as Islamic parties, their combined votes were 37.4 per cent, still lower compared to the 1955 election during which the combined votes for Islamic parties were about 43.5 per cent.[4] This may be interpreted that *Pancasila* as a pluralist ideology had been accepted by a majority of the Indonesian voters.

Despite the lower number of votes for Islamic parties, the influence of these parties grew after the fall of Soeharto. This was reflected in the presidential election of 1999 when Amien Rais, the leader of PAN,

TABLE 1.1
The 1999 Election Results for the DPR: Indonesia

Rank	Party	VOTES		SEATS	
		Number	Percentage	Number	Percentage
1	PDI-P	35,689,073	33.74	153	33.12
2	Golkar	23,741,749	22.44	120	25.97
3	PKB	13,336,982	12.61	51	11.04
4	PPP	11,329,905	10.71	58	12.55
5	PAN	7,528,956	7.12	34	7.36
6	PBB	2,049,708	1.94	13	2.81
7	PK	1,436,565	1.36	7	1.52
8	PKP	1,065,686	1.01	4	0.87
9	PNU	679,179	0.64	5	1.08
10	PDI	655,052	0.62	2	0.43
11	United	551,028	0.52	1	0.22
12	PDKB	550,846	0.52	5	1.08
13	PPIM	456,718	0.43	1	0.22
14	PDR	427,854	0.40	2	0.43
15	PNI	377,137	0.36	0	0.00
16	PSII	375,920	0.36	1	0.22
17	Krisna	369,719	0.35	0	0.00
18	PNI-FM	365,176	0.35	1	0.22
19	PBI	364,291	0.34	1	0.22
20	PNI-M	345,720	0.33	1	0.22
21	IPKI	328,564	0.31	1	0.22
22	PKU	300,064	0.28	1	0.22
23	Kami	289,489	0.27	0	0.00
24	PUI	269,309	0.25	0	0.00
25	PKD	216,675	0.20	0	0.00
26	Abul Yatama	213,979	0.20	0	0.00
27	Republik	208,157	0.20	0	0.00
28	MKGR	204,204	0.19	0	0.00
29	PIB	192,712	0.18	0	0.00
30	Suni	180,167	0.17	0	0.00
31	PCD	168,087	0.16	0	0.00
32	PSII-1905	152,820	0.14	0	0.00
33	New Masyumi	152,589	0.14	0	0.00
34	PNBI	149,136	0.14	0	0.00
35	PUDI	140,980	0.13	0	0.00
36	PBN	111,629	0.11	0	0.00
37	PKM	104,385	0.10	0	0.00
38	PND	96,984	0.09	0	0.00
39	PADI	85,838	0.08	0	0.00
40	PRD	78,727	0.07	0	0.00
41	PPI	63,934	0.06	0	0.00
42	PID	62,901	0.06	0	0.00
43	Murba	62,006	0.06	0	0.00
44	PSPSI	61,105	0.06	0	0.00
45	Pari	54,790	0.05	0	0.00
46	PUMI	49,839	0.05	0	0.00
47	PSP	49,807	0.05	0	0.00
48	Pilar	40,517	0.04	0	0.00
	TOTAL	105,786,658	100.00	462	100.00

Source: Compiled from Suryadinata (2001) and Komisi Pemilihan Umum (n.d.).

formed Poros Tengah (Central Axis), a grouping of Islamic parties in the MPR. In the 1999 election, the Indonesian president was elected by the MPR which consisted of DPR members, appointed military members and local representatives. Amien Rais succeeded in using his Poros Tengah to persuade a medium party leader, Abdurrahman Wahid (Gus Dur), to contest the presidential election against Megawati.

The April 2004 Election and Winning Parties

The political reform after 21 May 1998 also brought about the much larger number of parties desiring to contest the 2004 parliamentary election. More than 200 parties had initially registered at the Ministry of Justice and Human Rights. However, only 84 were willing to undergo administrative verification, resulting in only 50 legally recognized parties. Among these 50, six parties (the PDI-P, Golkar Party, PKB, PPP, PAN, and PBB) were automatically considered legal entities because they had passed the electoral threshold, while the remaining 44 had to undergo further administrative verification. Many were new parties contesting for the first time; some were old parties which had to re-register with different names as they did not pass the electoral threshold in 1999. For example, the PK was transformed into PKS and PIB to PPIB. Finally, after empirical and factual examination by the KPU (General Election Commission), only 24 parties were declared qualified to participate in the 2004 elections. Table 1.2 presents the list of parties according to the order of the sequence number given to them for the elections and factual verification. In terms of ideological orientations, 16 parties were based on the *Pancasila*, 5 parties on Islam, and 3 parties had other orientations.

The 5 April 2004 election was also the most complicated election as Indonesians had to vote for their representatives in the national (DPR), provincial (DPRD I), and district (DPRD II) parliaments in addition to DPD. This was the first step in a series of votes that culminated in the country's first direct election of the president and vice president. In addition, there was also a change in the way of casting the votes for these parliamentary elections (DPR and DPRDs). This change was aimed at reducing the possibility of using incorrect ways to punch the ballot paper that rendered the votes invalid.[5]

For this election, the IFES conducted a series of tracking surveys, starting its first wave in December 2003, after the KPU finished the registration process, verification, and affirmation of the participating twenty-four parties. The result of the first wave indicated that eight

TABLE 1.2

Profiles of 24 Parties Competing in the 2004 Elections

Sequence Number	Party Name and Its Acronym	Place and Date of Inception	Leader	Ideology	Factual Verification
1	Partai Nasional Indonesia Marhaenisme (PNI Marhaenisme, or Marhaenism Indonesian National Party)	Jakarta, 20 May 2002	DM Sukmawati Soekarnoputri	Marhaenism	24 provinces
2	Partai Buruh Sosial Demokrat (PBSD, or Socialist Democratic Labor Party)	Jakarta, 1 May 2001	Muchtar Pakpahan	Pancasila and UUD 1945	22 provinces
3	Partai Bulan Bintang (PBB, or Crescent Star Party)	Jakarta, 17 July 1998	Yusril Ihza Mahendra	Islam	Electoral threshold
4	Partai Merdeka (Freedom Party)	Jakarta, 10 October 2002	Adi Sasono	Pancasila	22 provinces
5	Partai Persatuan Pembangunan (PPP, or United Development Party)	Jakarta, 5 January 1973	Hamzah Haz	Islam	Electoral threshold
6	Partai Persatuan Demokrasi Kebangsaan (PPDK, or United Democratic Nationhood Party)	Jakarta, 23 July 2003	M Ryaas Rasyid	Pancasila	23 provinces
7	Partai Perhimpunan Indonesia Baru (PPIB, or New Indonesia Alliance Party)	Jakarta, 23 September 2002	Sjahrir	Justice, Democracy, Welfare	22 provinces
8	Partai Nasional Banteng Kemerdekaan (PNBK, or Freedom Bull National Party)	Jakarta, 27 July 2002	Eros Djarot	Marhaenism	21 provinces
9	Partai Demokrat (Democratic Party)	Jakarta, 9 September 2001	S Budhisantoso	Pancasila	25 provinces
10	Partai Keadilan dan Persatuan (PKP Indonesia, or Indonesian Justice and Unity Party)	Jakarta, 9 September 2002	Jend TNI (Purn) Edi Sudrajat	Pancasila	23 provinces
11	Partai Penegak Demokrasi Indonesia (PPDI, or Indonesian Democratic Vanguard Party)	Jakarta, 10 January 2003	H Dimmy Haryanto	Pancasila	21 provinces

No.	Party	Place, Date	Leader	Ideology	Status
12	Partai Persatuan Nahdlatul Ummah Indonesia (PPNUI, or Indonesian Nahdlatul Community Party)	Jakarta, 5 March 2003	KH Syukron Ma'mun	Islam	22 provinces
13	Partai Amanat Nasional (PAN, or National Mandate Party)	Jakarta, 23 August 1998	HM Amien Rais	Pancasila	Electoral threshold
14	Partai Karya Peduli Bangsa (PKPB, or Concern for the Nation Functional Party)	Jakarta, 9 September 2002	Jend TNI (Purn) HR Hartono	Pancasila	23 provinces
15	Partai Kebangkitan Bangsa (PKB, or National Awakening Party)	Jakarta, 23 July 1998	Alwi Abdurrahman Shihab	Pancasila	Electoral threshold
16	Partai Keadilan Sejahtera (PKS, or Prosperous Justice Party)	Jakarta, 20 April 2002	Hidayat Nur Wahid	Islam	23 provinces
17	Partai Bintang Reformasi (PBR, or Reform Star Party)	Jakarta, 20 January 2002	KH Zainuddin MZ	Islam	23 provinces
18	Partai Demokrasi Indonesia Perjuangan (PDI-P, or Indonesian Democratic Party of Struggle)	Jakarta, 10 January 1973	Megawati Soekarnoputri	Pancasila	Electoral threshold
19	Partai Damai Sejahtera (PDS, or Prosperous Peace Party)	Jakarta, 1 October 2001	Ruyandi Hutasoit	Pancasila	21 provinces
20	Partai Golkar (Golkar Party)	Jakarta, 20 October 1964	Akbar Tanjung	Pancasila	Electoral threshold
21	Partai Patriot Pancasila (Pancasila Patriots' Party)	Jakarta, 1 June 2001	KRMH Japto S Soerjosoemarno	Pancasila	21 provinces
22	Partai Sarikat Indonesia (PSI, or Indonesian Unity Party)	Surabaya, 17 December 2002	H Rahardjo Tjakraningrat	Pancasila	22 provinces
23	Partai Persatuan Daerah (PPD, or Regional United Party)	Jakarta, 18 November 2002	Oesman Sapta	Pancasila	21 provinces
24	Partai Pelopor (Pioneers' Party)	Jakarta, 29 November 2002	Rachmawati Soekarnoputri	Pancasila	21 provinces

Source: Compiled from <www.kpu.go.id/partai_partai/nourut.php>.

parties (Golkar, PDI-P, PAN, PKB, PPP, PKS, PBB and PD) were favoured by the respondents as the parties which could best represent their aspirations. It is interesting to note that the existence of PD, a new party, had been identified by the respondents.

According to results of several waves of tracking surveys conducted by the IFES, as seen in Figure 1.2, the Golkar and PDI-P, both *Pancasila* parties, had always been the two most favoured parties among these eight parties from December 2003 until March 2000, with Golkar, as always, the first winner, though each of them never had a single majority, or more than 50 per cent of the vote. Not surprisingly, the same pattern was seen in the official results of the parliamentary election in April 2004, where Golkar won the first position, followed by the PDI-P. Though still occupying only the second position, the PDI-P's performance in the election was much better than that before the election. Perhaps the fact that Megawati started to come closer to the people just before the elections had contributed to the PDI-P's improved position, though it had been too late to win.

In December 2003, the PD, a new *Pancasila* party, had emerged and occupied the lowest ranking among the eight parties and it was always

FIGURE 1.2

Parties Best Representing People's Aspirations: Indonesia, December 2003 – March 2004

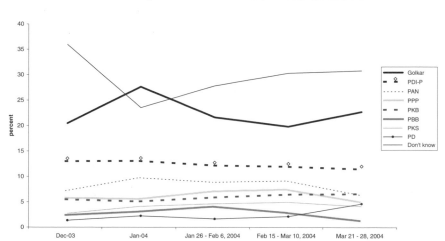

Source: Results from Wave I through IX of Tracking Survey (IFES, 2004*b*).

in the lowest position until early March 2004. However, the popularity of the PD, the party of Yudhoyono, had jumped to sixth position in late March 2004, about seven days away from the actual election. This sudden increase may be attributable to the fact that Yudhoyono had just declared himself as a candidate to run in the presidential race. The party's rising popularity continued during the election, where it finally reached the fifth position. The achievement of the PD was parallel to that of the PKS, an Islamic party and a small party (PK) in the 1999 election. It reached number 7 in December and managed to improve its standing to the sixth position in the election.

Most of about 150 million eligible voters went to the polls to cast their votes on 5 April 2004.[6] The Australian Parliamentary Observer Delegation commented that the polling days were much more a peaceful, calm, and friendly community-based feast. The implementation of the election was mostly orderly and well executed with excellent coordination. There were some minor violations such as officials helping some voters, especially the elderly, to cast a ballot paper, and voters handing the ballot to officials who then placed them in the ballot box.[7] Despite reports of some irregularities, the chief of the European Union Election Observer Mission said that they were minor. There was almost no incident across most of the country, though two Indonesian election officials were reported killed while delivering voting equipment in Papua. After a month of counting, on Wednesday, 5 May 2004, a one-week delay from the timeline,[8] the KPU announced the final election results, having counted 113.5 million valid votes and 11 million invalid ones. In other words, there were about 25.5 million Golput (GOLongan PUTih — "White Group") — people who did not use their right to vote — in the parliamentary election. Referred to as Golput were eligible voters who either did not register or registered but did not vote. This number of Golput could be higher if it included the invalid votes from people purposely punching the ballot paper in the wrong ways. With this conservative estimate, the number of Golput was larger than the number of votes for Golkar, the party that had won the most votes in 2004.

Golput is quite an interesting phenomenon in Indonesian politics, as it may be another sign of a rising democracy in Indonesia — participating in the election is not compulsory and being Golput is legal. This Golput, however, should be distinguished from the Golput in the New Order under Soeharto. In the New Order, Golput reflected an opposition to the government, whereas the current Golput may simply mean that none of the candidates matched the aspirations of a particular voter (who chose to be a Golput).[9]

As in 1999, the results presented in Figure 1.3 show that there was also no single majority winner, that is, with more than 50 per cent of the vote, in the 2004 parliamentary election. Major parties of 1999 survived during the 2004 election, but the percentages of their votes decreased. Most obvious was the PDI-P which suffered a severe decline from 33.7 per cent in 1999 to 18.5 per cent in 2004. Golkar secured the second position in 1999, and managed to be the first winner in 2004 — yet, the percentage obtained (21.6 per cent) was still lower than its gain in the previous election (22.5 per cent). In other words, compared to 1999, the 2004 landscape of the political parties was more fragmented, and large parties were less dominant.

FIGURE 1.3
Results of the 2004 Parliamentary Election: Indonesia

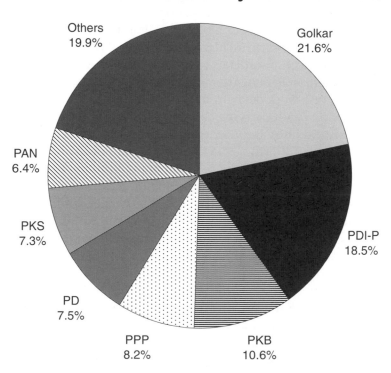

Source: Calculated from Table 1.3.

Noteworthy is the shrinking number of parties which claim Islam as their ideological basis. Out of the 24 parties that contested in the 2004 elections, 5 were Islamic parties (PPP, PBB, PKS, PBR, and PPNUI) in contrast to 18 out of 48 parties in 1999; the absolute majority was always *Pancasila* parties. A comparison between the numbers of Islamic parties in 1999 and 2004 shows a relative stability — political Islam remains a minority in the Indonesian political scene. They have not even managed to recover the 43 per cent of the total vote in the 1955 election. In the 1999 election, the combined votes for the 18 Islamic parties constituted 17.7 per cent — or 37.4 per cent if the PKB and PAN are considered to be "Islamic parties" — while in 2004, the combined votes of the 5 Islamic parties formed 21.2 per cent — or 39.4 per cent if the PKB and PAN are included. It should be noted here that the PKB and PAN officially declared themselves as *Pancasila* parties, but because their main constituents, especially the PAN, were Muslims, these two parties were often seen as Islamic parties. In other words, nationalist and secular parties are still more favoured by the voters, and the domination of political Islam remains to be seen.

The rising number of votes for the Islamic parties was mainly contributed by the emergence of the PKS, which dramatically rose in popularity from 1.4 per cent of the votes in 1999 to 7.3 per cent of the votes in 2004. The PPP, an Islamic party during the authoritarian regime, lost its popularity, decreasing from 10.7 per cent in 1999 to 8.2 per cent in 2004. Like the PPP, two other major Islamic parties (the PKB and PAN) also experienced declining popularity in the 2004 elections.

To win the second round of the presidential elections, politicians had to build coalitions and two coalitions of political parties were formed. On the one hand, there were three old established parties (Golkar, PDI-P, and PPP) and a new and small party (PDS) forming the National Coalition (Koalisi Kebangsaan) to support the Megawati–Hasyim nomination. On the other hand, on 26 August 2004, the PD, PBB, PKPI, and PKS declared the People's Coalition (Koalisi Kerakyatan) to back the nomination of Yudhoyono–Kalla.

With the formation of these two coalitions, the dichotomy between *Pancasila* and Islamic parties became blurred. The National Coalition consisted of three *Pancasila* parties (42.24 per cent) and one Islamic party (8.15 per cent), while the People's Coalition comprised two *Pancasila* parties (8.71 per cent) and two Islamic parties (9.96 per cent). The PBR, another Islamic party, with 2.4 per cent of the votes, gave its moral support to the National Coalition. At the same time, two *Pancasila* parties with Muslims as their constituents,

TABLE 1.3
The 2004 Election Results for the DPR: Indonesia

Rank	Party	VOTES		SEATS		
		Number	Percent	Number	Percent	MK
1	GOLKAR	24,480,757	21.58	128	23.27	128
2	PDI-P	21,026,629	18.53	109	19.82	109
3	PKB	11,989,564	10.57	52	9.45	52
4	PPP	9,248,764	8.15	58	10.55	58
5	PD	8,455,225	7.45	57	10.36	55
6	PKS	8,325,020	7.34	45	8.18	45
7	PAN	7,303,324	6.44	52	9.45	53
8	PBB	2,970,487	2.62	11	2.00	11
9	PBR	2,764,998	2.44	13	2.36	14
10	PDS	2,414,254	2.13	12	2.18	13
11	PKPB	2,399,290	2.11	2	0.36	2
12	PKPI	1,424,240	1.26	1	0.18	1
13	PPDK	1,313,654	1.16	5	0.91	4
14	PNBK	1,230,455	1.08	1	0.18	0
15	PANCASILA	1,073,139	0.95	0	0.00	0
16	PNIM	923,159	0.81	1	0.18	1
17	PPNUI	895,610	0.79	0	0.00	0
18	PP	878,932	0.77	2	0.36	3
19	PPDI	855,811	0.75	1	0.18	1
20	MERDEKA	842,541	0.74	0	0.00	0
21	PSI	679,296	0.6	0	0.00	0
22	PPIB	672,952	0.59	0	0.00	0
23	PPD	657,916	0.58	0	0.00	0
24	PBSD	636,397	0.56	0	0.00	0
	TOTAL	113,462,414	100.00	550	100.00	550

Note: MK – Mahkamah Konstitusi (Constitutional Court) that is tasked with settling disputes arising from election results. This column lists the number of seats after all disputes were settled.
Source: Table 1 in Wiratma (2004).

the PKB and PAN, provided their moral support to the People's Coalition, contributing 17.0 per cent of the votes. It is, however, interesting to note that after Megawati was defeated in the second round, the PPP withdrew from the National Coalition. The replacement of Akbar Tanjung by Jusuf Kalla, the new vice president, as the general chairman of Golkar in December 2004 made the National Coalition more uncertain, as Golkar under Kalla may no longer honour the coalition against the Yudhoyono administration.

Emergence of New Parties

In the 2004 elections, two "new" parties, the Partai Demokrat (PD, 7.5 per cent) and Partai Keadilan Sejahtera (PKS, 7.3 per cent) garnered a total of 14.8 per cent of the votes. The PD was fifth-placed and PKS sixth. They may play important roles in the future politics. The emergence of these two stars contributed to the decline of the percentage of votes gained by the major "old" parties. The rise of the PD, with *Pancasila* as the ideology and perceived as a secular party, was perhaps at the expense of Golkar and PDI-P. On the other hand, the rising popularity of the PKS, an Islamic party, might have also curtailed the votes for the PPP, PBB, and PAN.

Partai Demokrat (PD)

The PD is closely linked to retired General Susilo Bambang Yudhoyono, who was coordinating minister for security during both the Gus Dur and Megawati cabinets. Many secular nationalists considered Yudhoyono as a potential future leader. Way back in 2001, after the removal of Gus Dur and the appointment of Megawati to succeed Gus Dur as the president, these secular nationalists in the MPR proposed Yudhoyono as the vice president, but he came in third after Hamzah Haz of the PPP and Akbar Tanjung of Golkar.

Nevertheless, the nationalists did not give up; they saw the future in this former military general. A group of intellectuals (including many university professors) and professionals decided to establish a party, the PD, for Yudhoyono. Yudhoyono himself did not hold any formal position in the party, but his wife, Kristiani Herawati, was the deputy chairperson. Kristiani is a daughter of General Sarwo Edhie Wibowo, who was the most high-profile commander of Special Forces (Kopassus) between 1965 and 1967.

The chairman of the party is Dr Subur Budhisantoso, a professor in the Department of Anthropology at the University of Indonesia. Within a short period of time, the party was able to establish branches in all major provinces. The founders were inspired by Thaksin Shinawatra's Thai Rak Thai party, a new party which emerged overnight as a ruling party. They hoped that the PD as a new party would emerge as the governing party in the elections.[10]

The PD favours the unitary state of Indonesia and advocates cultural pluralism. It also preaches democracy and advocates popular political participation and a professional army. It wants to combat corruption and nepotism; it is against violence. In post-Soeharto Indonesia, where corruption and violence have been rampant, the emergence of the PD was a breath of fresh air and attracted many educated urban voters.

As a new party, the PD was not taken seriously at first. However, it received a stimulus when Megawati refused to let Yudhoyono, then her coordinating minister for security, attend a cabinet meeting. Yudhoyono subsequently withdrew from her cabinet. This proved a blessing in disguise for the PD, which gained a lot of sympathy votes as a result.

Partai Keadilan Sejahtera (PKS)

Another "new star" in this election, the PKS, was not really new. In the 1999 election, it was called Partai Keadilan (PK) and won 1.34 per cent of the votes. It was the seventh largest party but failed to pass the electoral threshold of 2 per cent. It changed its name to Partai Keadilan Sejahtera (PKS) for the 2004 elections.

PKS' constituents are Muslims, unlike the PD's constituents comprising both Muslims and non-Muslims. The ideology of PKS is Islam, and it states in the party vision that the PKS "strives for Islam as the solution for the [problems] in the national and state life" of Indonesia (Lubis 2004). The PKS also states in its programme that it strives to build an Indonesian society in accordance with the teachings of Allah "within the context of the unitary state of Indonesia which is based on *Pancasila*".[11]

The PKS of 2004 had a different strategy from that in 1999 when it was known as Partai Keadilan (PK). Instead of focusing on *syari'ah* law, the PKS stressed anti-corruption and anti-poverty in their campaign — this appealed to many urban dwellers, especially in Jakarta, the capital city of Indonesia. Some observers maintained that voters chose the PKS not because they wanted an Islamic state but because they supported the anti-corruption and anti-poverty promises that the PKS highlighted.

The leader of the PKS, Dr Hidayat Nur Wahid, received a thorough Islamic education, first at local Islamic institutions in Java, and later in the Madinah Islamic University in Saudi Arabia, from where he obtained his B.A. (1983), M.A. (1987) and Ph.D. (1992) in Islamic theology and law (Lubis 2004). He has been teaching in Islamic colleges in Indonesia since returning in 1992. He replaced Dr Ir Nur Mahmud Ismail in 2000 and led the new party to victory in the 2004 elections.

Partai Damai Sejahtera (PDS)

Another new and rising party in 2004 was the Partai Damai Sejahtera (PDS or Prosperous Peace Party), relying on support from minority groups. It is based on *Pancasila*, with Christians as their main constituents. It vows not to play money politics, but to take the lead as a moral force. As reported by Setiogi (2004), Ruyandi Hutasoit said, "We start within ourselves. PDS executives must be financially stable, otherwise they will be prone to corruption and enriching their families if they win legislative seats." Ruyandi Hutasoit is the party leader, a priest, a doctor, and the chairperson of the Doulos Foundation in Jakarta.

The PDS is similar to the PKB and PAN in terms of ideology in that all profess to be *Pancasila* parties and claim to be inclusive and pluralistic. However, the PKB and PAN have Muslims as their constituents and are perceived as Islamic parties, while the PDS has Christians as its constituents and is seen as a Christian party. The PDS is also similar to the PKS: both have voters with religious orientation as their main constituents, but during the campaigns they emphasized clean government and refrained from talking about issues related to religion.

The PDS aimed to fulfil the 3 per cent electoral threshold required to contest the presidential elections. However, it only managed to secure 2.1 per cent of the votes, or 2.4 million votes, at the national level, indicating that the majority of Christians did not vote for the PDS.

Splits within Major Parties

As stated earlier, several major parties lost votes in 2004. A contributing factor was the internal conflict that caused splits within the parties themselves.

PDI-P

It was after the 1999 election that the PDI-P suffered from splits. Megawati's younger sisters established their own parties to challenge the PDI-P: Sukmawati Soekarnoputri formed the PNI Marhaenisme or Marhaenisme Indonesian National Party, gaining 0.81 per cent.

Rachmawati Soekarnoputri, another sister of Megawati, established the Partai Pelopor or Pioneers' Party, obtaining 0.77 per cent. Eros Djarot, a former advisor and speechwriter of Megawati, also formed the Partai Nasional Banteng Kemerdekaan (PNBK or Freedom Bull National Party), gaining 1.08 per cent. It should be noted that that the PDI-P was actually a transformation of the "old" PDI (Partai Demokrasi Indonesia), and that the "old" PDI was changed to the PPDI (Partai Penegak Demokrasi Indonesia or Indonesian Democratic Vanguard Party). It contested in the 2004 elections, as a challenge to the PDI-P, though it only secured 0.75 per cent. The chairman of this new party was H. Dimmy Haryanto. Although these parties were unable to gain seats during the 2004 elections, there was no doubt that, to a certain extent, they took away the PDI-P votes.

Golkar

Golkar also suffered from several splits. Retired General Edi Sudrajat, who had left Golkar and established the PKP prior to the 1999 election, changed the name of the party to the PKPI (Partai Keadilan dan Persatuan Indonesia or Indonesian Justice and Unity Party) that challenged Golkar in the 2004 parliamentary election. It obtained 1.26 per cent of the votes. Another retired general, H.R. Hartono, created his own party, the PKPB (Partai Karya Peduli Bangsa or Concerned Nation Functional Party) in 2002. Hartono, the chairperson, had signalled that the party would nominate Siti Hardianti Rukmana (better known as Tutut), Soeharto's eldest daughter, as the presidential candidate. By nominating Tutut, the PKPB attempted to project an image of the "good old days", to woo voters who were frustrated with the current *Reformasi*. It gained 2.11 per cent of the votes. Another breakaway was KRMH Yapto Sulistio Soerjosoemarno, who was well-connected with the military. He formed the Partai Patriot Pancasila or Pancasila Patriots' Party that won 0.95 per cent of the votes. These splinter groups obviously contributed to the decline in the number of votes for Golkar, although not by much.

PPP

The PPP also experienced a split. K.H. Zainuddin MZ (better known as *Dai Sejuta Umat* — Cleric with One Million Followers) established the Partai Bintang Reformasi (PBR, or Reformed Star Party). K.H. Zainuddin, who created and chaired the PBR, insisted that it was not a split from the PPP, claiming that he started his political career in the PPP because he was curious why no Islamic-based party could win in the elections.

However, the fact was that he was a PPP leader who had quit the party and established a new one, called the PPP Reformasi (Reformed PPP Party) on 20 January 2002. Later it was renamed PBR, during the Extraordinary Congress on 8–9 April 2003 in Jakarta. It secured 2.44 per cent of the votes in the 2004 elections. Apparently this was at the expense of the PPP.

PKB
The PKB also suffered a potential conflict when Matori Abdul Djalil, the chairman of NU and Minister for Defence, formed a separate party. However, the General Election Committee decided that the party of Matori was not eligible to contest in the 2004 parliamentary elections, as the Matori party was challenged by another group.

PAN
There was also an internal split within PAN after the 1999 election. Initially, PAN was meant to include members from various religious and political persuasions. However, it was later reported that the "radical" Islamic faction led by A.M. Fatwa won. As a consequence, moderates such as Faisal Basri left the party. Although those who left the party did not form their own, there was nevertheless a drift of non-Islamic leaders away from the party in early 2001. Bearing in mind that the main constituents of PAN were the educated urban Muslim voters, the rise of the PKS (that also appeals to urban Muslim voters) might have been an important competitor for PAN.

The New Parliament (DPR) and Assembly (MPR)

Twenty-four parties contested in the April 2004 election, of which only sixteen parties won at least one parliamentary seat (see Table 1.4), while eight parties secured none: the PNBK, PBSD, Merdeka Party, PPIB, PPNU, Pancasila Party, PSI and PPD.

Golkar secured the largest number of seats (128 seats), followed by the PDI-P (109 seats), PPP (58 seats), PD (55 seats), PAN (53 seats), PKB (52 seats), PKS (45 seats), PBR (14 seats), PDS (13 seats) and PBB (11 seats). However, this was not the order of the number of votes the parties gained during the elections. According to the number of votes, the order of the parties should be as follows: Golkar, PDI-P, PKB, PPP, PD, PKS, PAN, PBB, PBR and PDS. The "discrepancy" was due to the special election method in order to address the issue of uneven

TABLE 1.4

Number of Seats Gained by the Major and Medium Parties: 1999 and 2004 Election Results

No.	Party	1999[a]	2004[b]
1	PDI-P	153	109
2	Golkar	120	128
3	PKB	51	52
4	PPP	58	58
5	PAN	34	53
6	PBB	13	11
7	PKS or PK in 1999	7	45
8	PD	–	55
9	PBR	–	14
10	PDS	–	13
11	PKPB	–	2
	Other parties	26[c]	10[d]
	Total	462	550

Source: a. Compiled from Komisi Pemilihan Umum (1999).
    b. Table 1.3.
    c. This number consists of 5 seats for each of PDKB and PNU, 4 seats for PKP, 2 seats for each of PDI and PDR, and 1 seat for each of the other eight parties.
    d. This number consists of 4 seats of PPDK, 3 seats of PP, 1 seat of each of these parties (PKPI, PPDI and PNIM).

population distribution in Java and the Outer Islands. Sherlock (2004) mentioned that with the new rule, Java could have a maximum of 55 per cent of the seats, whereas in 1999 it could only have a maximum of 50 per cent.

Allocation of Parliamentary Seats: A New System

The method used for the allocation of seats to the political parties was called the "Largest Remainder". The allocated seats in the electoral district were distributed into the political parties in two stages. In the first stage, the valid votes gained by each party in the electoral district were divided by the BPP to gain full quota seats. The BPP (*Bilangan Pembagi Pemilihan* or quota) is the value of a seat, showing the number of votes for one seat. The BPP was calculated by dividing the total number of valid votes in the electoral district by the number of the total allocated seats in the district. Therefore, only parties gaining numbers of votes more than the BPP will automatically secure the seats.

Some parties did not get any seats at all, because their numbers of votes were smaller than the BPP. Others had seats, but they still had some remaining votes not sufficiently large to produce one additional seat.

The second stage dealt with the remaining votes, which were insufficient to secure seats in the first stage. The remaining allocated seats, after subtracting the full quota seats in the first stage, were distributed to the political parties based on the rank order of their remaining votes. Finally, the number of seats produced in the first and second stages were added to obtain the total number of seats gained by each party.

Because Java is more populous than the Outer Islands, the BPP for electoral districts in the Outer Islands were "cheaper", that is, requiring fewer votes to obtain one seat, than those in Java. In other words, the seats in some provinces in the Outer Islands could be gained by fewer votes than those in Java. On average, as shown in Table 1.5, the value of a seat in Java was more "expensive" (about 232,000 votes), than in the Outer Islands, where only about 173,000 votes were required.

As a consequence, the party that gained votes mostly from Java would probably gain a smaller number of seats because they would likely gain more "full-quota" seats than the "remaining" seats. For example, the PKB, which gained 87.5 per cent of its votes from Java, gained only 52 seats with votes of nearly 12.0 million. However, the PAN with only nearly 5 million votes, fewer than the PKB, gained even more seats (53) than the PKB. This is because the PKB gained 28 seats from its stronghold province, East Java, where the value of a seat was even more expensive (239,000 votes) than the average value in Java. Furthermore, these seats consisted of 21 full-quota seats. In Central Java, the second largest contributor of seats for the PKB, the party gained 13 seats, seven of them being full-quota seats. Therefore, more than 50 per cent of the PKB seats were full quota and expensive seats. In contrast, PAN seats consisted of only 4 full quota seats and 49 seats gained from the "remaining" votes.

If the seat allocation is compared to the 1999 election, the parliamentary seats for Golkar in the period of 2004–09 were 128 seats, an increase from 120 seats in the previous election. The PDI-P finished behind Golkar with 109 seats, down from the 153 seats in 1999. PPP won 58 seats to finish third, similar to its showing in the 1999 election. PAN did extremely well, achieving greater representation in parliament with 53 seats, 19 more than in the 1999 election. Similarly, the PKS enjoyed success with 45 seats, a dramatic increase from the 7 seats gained in the previous election (under the name of PK).

TABLE 1.5

The Value of a Seat (BPP) by Electoral District: Indonesia, 2004

		JAVA		
No.	Electoral District	Number of valid votes	Allocated Seats	BPP
1	Jakarta - I	2,645,455	12	220,455
2	Jakarta - II	2,091,197	9	232,355
3	West Java - I	1,551,512	6	258,585
4	West Java - II	2,257,385	10	225,739
5	West Java - III	2,365,665	11	215,060
6	West Java - IV	2,407,782	11	218,889
7	West Java - V	2,639,912	12	219,993
8	West Java - VI	1,436,132	6	239,355
9	West Java - VII	2,094,194	9	232,688
10	West Java - VIII	2,077,476	8	259,685
11	West Java - IX	1,514,752	7	216,393
12	West Java - X	2,357,645	10	235,765
13	Yogyakarta	1,924,647	8	240,581
14	Central Java - I	1,872,556	8	234,070
15	Central Java - II	1,494,440	7	213,491
16	Central Java - III	2,118,528	9	235,392
17	Central Java - IV	1,555,198	6	259,200
18	Central Java - V	1,976,172	8	247,022
19	Central Java - VI	2,002,563	8	250,320
20	Central Java - VII	1,549,330	7	221,333
21	Central Java - VIII	1,750,012	8	218,752
22	Central Java - IX	1,713,807	8	214,226
23	Central Java - X	1,599,200	7	228,457
24	East Java - I	2,314,090	10	231,409
25	East Java - II	1,667,135	7	238,162
26	East Java - III	1,722,167	7	246,024
27	East Java - IV	1,874,336	8	234,292
28	East Java - V	1,858,674	8	232,334
29	East Java - VI	2,255,615	9	250,624
30	East Java - VII	2,029,262	8	253,658
31	East Java - VIII	2,349,515	10	234,952
32	East Java - IX	2,653,113	11	241,192
33	East Java - X	1,834,891	8	229,361
34	Banten - I	2,065,831	11	187,803
35	Banten - II	2,315,957	11	210,542
	Total	69,936,146	303	
	Mean			232,233

Source: Compiled from <www.kpu.go.id>.

TABLE 1.5 – cont'd

	OUTER ISLANDS			
No.	Electoral District	Number of valid votes	Allocated Seats	BPP
36	N. Aceh Darussalam - I	1,149,898	7	164,271
37	N. Aceh Darussalam - II	955,579	6	159,263
38	North Sumatra - I	2,043,468	10	204,347
39	North Sumatra - II	1,633,466	9	181,496
40	North Sumatra - III	1,861,802	10	186,180
41	West Sumatra - I	1,142,019	8	142,752
42	West Sumatra - II	868,526	6	144,754
43	Riau	2,066,708	11	187,883
44	Jambi	1,278,080	7	182,583
45	South Sumatra - I	1,471,256	8	183,907
46	South Sumatra - II	1,898,544	8	237,318
47	Bengkulu	752,696	4	188,174
48	Lampung - I	1,614,206	8	201,776
49	Lampung - II	1,960,316	9	217,813
50	Bangka-Belitung	478,748	3	159,583
51	Riau Archipelago	566,126	3	188,709
52	Bali	1,904,600	9	211,622
53	West Nusa Tenggara	2,010,517	10	201,052
54	East Nusa Tenggara - I	950,073	6	158,346
55	East Nusa Tenggara - II	1,099,822	7	157,117
56	West Kalimantan	1,877,409	10	187,741
57	Central Kalimantan	874,163	6	145,694
58	South Kalimantan	1,557,199	11	141,564
59	East Kalimantan	1,346,699	7	192,386
60	North Sulawesi	1,201,938	6	200,323
61	Central Sulawesi	1,119,319	6	186,553
62	South Sulawesi - I	2,074,524	12	172,877
63	South Sulawesi - II	2,091,809	12	174,317
64	Southeast Sulawesi	894,886	5	178,977
65	Gorontalo	479,632	3	159,877
66	Maluku	658,037	4	164,509
67	Maluku Utara	413,983	3	137,994
68	West Irian Jaya	285,032	3	95,011
69	Papua	945,188	10	94,519
35	Banten - II	2,315,957	11	210,542
		43,526,268	247	
				173,273

The allocation of seats was not without its problems. When the KPU announced the results of seat allocation during a plenary session, it was signed by only ten out of twenty-four political parties.[12] The ten were PD, PPNUI, PPP, PPDK (United Democratic Nationhood Party), PAN, PKPB (Concern for the Nation Functional Party), PDI-P, PDS, Pancasila Patriot Party, and Golkar Party. An alliance of fourteen parties refused to accept the election results. The constitutional court received 131 complaints linked to the 5 April legislative election. Twenty-two complaints were filed by political parties.[13] Most of the cases revolved around disputes over ballot counting.

Finally, the Constitutional Court (MK or Mahkamah Konstitusi) settled the disputes on 21 June 2004.[14] Four political parties gained additional seats at the expense of other political parties (see Table 1.3). The Prosperous Peace Party (PDS) took an additional seat in the West Irian Jaya constituency after winning its dispute with the PPDK. In Papua, the PD had to let go one seat to the Pioneer Party. The only seat gained by the Freedom Bull National Party (PNBK) in West Kalimantan had to be handed over to the PBR. PAN gained one additional seat from Central Sulawesi at the expense of the PD.

The Members and Leaders

Out of 550 members of the new 2004–09 parliament or DPR, over 70 per cent are new faces. In terms of educational level, at least 70 per cent of the present DPR members are university graduates (see Appendix 1). The education composition varies across parties. Among Golkar members, the largest party, about 32 per cent are postgraduates, and nearly three quarters have at least undergraduate education. More than half or 57 per cent of the PDI-P members are university graduates. PAN MPs have the highest educational qualification and in fact about 85 per cent of them are university graduates. This percentage is higher than the percentage of PKS (67 per cent). All eleven members of the PBB faction are university graduates.

The number of women in the DPR is supposed to be 30 per cent but as in the 1999 election, the 2004 election results did not meet the target. However, the number of women in the parliament increased from 43 in the 1999 to 61 in 2004. In other words, this was an increase from 9.3 per cent of elected members in 1999 to 11.1 per cent in 2004 (Sherlock 2004).

The new members of the DPR and the DPD were finally sworn in during a ceremony overseen by Supreme Court Chief Justice, Bagir Manan, on 1 October 2004. President Megawati Soekarnoputri and Vice

President Hamzah Haz also attended the ceremony. Three new members of the DPR were absent from the ceremony: two Golkar legislators, Fahmi Idris and Marzuki Darusman, who had just been dismissed from Golkar, and Anwar bin Marzuki of the PPP who had been disqualified from serving in the House after being found guilty of using a fake diploma in the elections (Hari 2004).

The National Coalition reached an agreement to back Golkar Party candidate, Agung Laksono, for the post of Speaker of the DPR,[15] while the People's Coalition nominated Endin Sofihara of the PPP. Four lawmakers abstained, while six votes were declared invalid during the elections. The PPP, which forsook the National Coalition, had finally joined the People's Coalition. Finally, the People's Coalition lost the DPR leadership election on Saturday, 2 October 2004, as Agung was elected as the speaker of the house. Agung, a senior Golkar politician, garnered 280 votes to beat Endin Sofihara,[16] with only 257 votes. Agung's deputy speakers are Soetardjo Soerjogoeritno of the PDI-P, Muhaimin Iskandar of the PKB and Zainal Maarif of the Reform Star Party (PBR).

One day before the election of Agung Laksono, on 1 October 2004, Ginandjar Kartasasmita, a DPD member from West Java, was elected as the inaugural speaker of the DPD,[17] defeating Irman Gusman from the DPD West Sumatra in a run-off.[18] Ginandjar received 72 votes while Irman gained 54 votes. One voter abstained and one vote was invalid. Irman Gusman and La Ode Ida became Ginandjar's deputies.

The MPR members were initially scheduled to elect their leaders on Saturday, 2 October 2004, but all that happened was a series of protracted meetings and intense lobbying after the 124-strong DPD demanded a revision of the MPR's standing orders with regard to the election mechanism. The DPR had initially insisted that three of the assembly's four leaders should come from its members, while the DPD wanted the leaders to come evenly from the house and the DPD. Claiming they had an equal right to be involved in the nomination of candidates, the DPD members proposed that both the DPR and the DPD be given the right to nominate two candidates each, with a vote being held to ultimately decide on the assembly's leadership. The MPR members finally agreed to have two candidates from each house.

The People's Coalition eventually won the People's Consultative Assembly (MPR) leadership election. Hidayat Nur Wahid, the chairperson of the PKS, snatched the assembly's speakership in a hair-splitting race against Sutjipto of the National Coalition. Hidayat grabbed 326 votes, while Sutjipto secured 324 votes. Elected as Hidayat's deputies were A.M. Fatwa of PAN and two members of the DPD — Moeryati Soedibyo and M. Aksa Mahmud. The People's Coalition victory came as a surprise as the National Coalition members initially wanted the PDI-P candidate to be the speaker for the MPR. The National Coalition fielded Sutjipto as assembly speaker and Theo L. Sambuaga of Golkar, DPD members Sarwono Kusumaatmadja from DPD Jakarta, and Aida Ismeth from Riau DPD as deputies. With the election of Hidayat from the People's Coalition, which supports Yudhoyono–Kalla, as the chairperson of the MPR, any move to impeach Yudhoyono–Kalla is likely to be thwarted by the MPR.

Concluding Remarks

The 1999 and particularly 2004 parliamentary elections have indicated that democracy has been emerging in Indonesia. Despite the problems faced in printing ballot papers and delayed distribution of the materials such as ballot papers, ballot boxes, and voting screens, many observers concluded that the election process was generally orderly, well coordinated and well run. A three-week campaign period and election day itself were relatively peaceful and smooth. The relative peacefulness and smoothness of the process are themselves an achievement for Indonesia which has just emerged from an authoritarian rule in 1998. Though democracy is still in its infancy, the gigantic, complicated, process of the 2004 elections has generally resulted in a more democratic Indonesia.

The political party system in Indonesia has remained plural in the last five years and will remain plural if there is no sudden collapse of the government. There has been more continuity than change in parliament. The six largest parties from the 1999 election survived in the 2004 elections. Furthermore, in the 1999 election three major parties (the PDI-P, Golkar and the PKB) gained more than 10 per cent of the vote, and these three parties remained as the top three in the 2004 elections. However, the order changed; Golkar regained its victory as the top party replacing the PDI-P. Like the PDI-P in 1999, Golkar was also unable to reach a majority position in the parliament.

In the 2004 elections, voters articulated their dissatisfaction towards the old parties and put their future in the parties symbolizing change for the better. As a result, the five old parties (Golkar, PDI-P, PKB, PPP, and PAN) suffered declining support in the last five years. The parties in 2004 were more fragmented than in 1999. In 2004, the political landscape saw a larger number of players.

The PDI-P had undergone a serious setback, losing 15.3 percentage points of the votes. The PKB and PAN failed to broaden their support. The PPP, an Islamic party, was also unable to get support from the majority Muslims. The PBB was the only older, and the smallest, party which enjoyed an increase in the percentage of support. The reasons for the decline in support among the five old parties are complex, but three major factors can be identified: voters' unhappiness with the old, established, parties; emergence of new rival parties; and splits within major parties.

The PD and PKS are two rising stars; the former is secular and the latter is Islamic. Both may become major actors in the 2009 elections. Yet, the two parties were quite different in the ways they impressed the electorate. The PD is interesting, as it appears that declining support for both Golkar and especially the PDI-P may have been partly attributed to the emergence of the PD. It is possible that its future growth will be at the expense of Golkar and the PDI-P. The PKS as an Islamic party may challenge the existing Islamic parties, especially the PPP, PAN, and PBB.

Of interest is the dichotomy between secularism and Islam. In both the 1999 and 2004 elections, the secular parties, or more properly, the *Pancasila* parties, emerged as the majority while Islamic parties remained as the minority. Also, during the 2004 parliamentary election, Islam was not an issue. All political parties, including Islamic parties, were focusing on issues other than religion. The vast majority of Indonesian Muslims seem far more concerned with economic recovery, eradicating corruption, and bringing social stability back to their lives than pursuing any agenda on the implementation of *syari'ah* into the state law.

Not surprisingly, the dichotomy in parliament is not between the *Pancasila* and Islamic parties, but between the National Coalition and People's Coalition. It is true that the National Coalition consists of mostly *Pancasila* parties, but the People's Coalition also includes *Pancasila* parties and some parties with Muslim constituents that also embrace *Pancasila* as their ideology.

In short, with the new electoral system as discussed in this book's Introduction, and the relatively free, fair, and peaceful process of the parliamentary election in 2004, democracy has been born in Indonesia. Democracy can emerge in a country with Muslims constituting around 88 per cent of the population without having Islamic parties controlling the country. Democracy as being practised in Indonesia is far from perfect, but it has gone beyond the national level. The laws on regional autonomy implemented in 2001 have brought significant changes to Indonesian districts and provinces. The next chapter discusses regional variations of the 2004 parliamentary election.

Notes

1. For more detailed discussions on the socio-economic determinants of voting behaviour in the 1999 elections, see Ananta, Arifin, and Suryadinata (2004).
2. "Partai-Partai Politik Indonesia: Ideologi, Strategi dan Program", *Kompas*, 1999, p. 412.
3. In 1999 there were 30 *Pancasila* parties and 18 Islamic parties. The Islamic parties were PPP, PIB, KAMI, PUI, PKU, PMB, PSII, PAY, PSII-1905, PPIM, PBB, PK, PNUI, PID, PP, PCD, PSUNI and PUMI. PAN and PKB declared they were *Pancasila* parties but were often perceived as Islamic parties because Muslims were their main constituents.
4. It consisted of 20.9 per cent of the vote for Masyumi, 18.4 per cent for NU, 2.9 per cent for PSII and 1.3 per cent for Perti.
5. In the previous election, the correct way to vote was to punch one party symbol only. In 2004, a voter punched one party and at the same time punched a candidate from the same party — this is an important feature of the 2004 elections, having an open list of candidates. The vote was not valid if a voter only picked a candidate. The size of the ballot paper was as big as a newspaper. In addition, the voters also voted for a new legislative body, the DPD, in which they had to vote for one candidate only — there was no party affiliation for the DPD candidates. These new features had resulted in confusion among some voters.

   An indication of this confusion among the eligible voters was noticed in the first of the IFES tracking surveys, conducted in 13–18 December 2003.[5] It showed the voters' knowledge of procedure for the April 2004 election, and it revealed that 64 per cent of respondents correctly cited punching one party symbol as a valid vote, as this was the way they used to vote in previous election. However, only 13 per cent of the respondents knew that they had an option to also vote for one candidate from the same party. The results of the survey also show that 40 per cent of the respondents knew of the DPD, a new body. Of those aware of it, 52 per cent were aware that the proper way to vote for the DPD was to select only one candidate. This may indicate unawareness of the new feature of the April elections.

   However, as time moved along with the efforts to educate the voters, the ninth wave of the tracking survey conducted between 21 and 28 March 2004, about one week before the actual voting, revealed an exceptionally large increase on this knowledge. Twenty-three per cent of respondents correctly cited punching one party symbol only. In addition, 66 per cent of the respondents were able to identify the punching for one party as well as one candidate from the same party they selected. In other words, close to 90 per cent of the voters knew how to cast a valid vote for the parliament. Awareness of the DPD had also increased to 58 per cent. Of those aware of it, 84 per cent were knowledgeable on casting a valid vote by selecting only one candidate.

6. Eligible voters are the citizens of Indonesia aged 17 years old and over. Unfortunately, it has been difficult to find exact information on the number of eligible voters in the 2004 elections. Therefore, we make our own estimation, using the data from the 2000 population census and using some judgements on the rate of growth during 2000–04 for the population aged 17 and above. We came up with a conservative estimate of 150 million eligible voters — it can be higher than 150 million. If it is higher, then the number of Golput is higher too.

7. More detailed reports on the election are referred to by the Parliament of the Commonwealth of Australia (2004).

8. Here is the timeline of the 2004 elections:

15 March–1 April	Active campaigning for legislature candidates/parties (DPR, DPRD and DPD)
2–4 April	"Quiet time"
5 April	Elections for legislature — declared a national holiday
21–30 April	Announcement of results followed by allocation of seats
1 June–1 July	Presidential campaign
2–4 July	"Quiet time"
5 July	Presidential election
26 July	Announcement of results (If no clear winner of the Presidential election appears, a second "run-off" will be held)
14–16 September	Active campaigning
20 September	Presidential run-off election
5 October	Announcement of results
20 October	Inauguration of president and vice president

9. For a study on the origin and development of Golput, see Arbi Sanit, ed., *Aneka Pandangan Fenomena Politik* (Jakarta: Pustaka Sinar Harapan, 1992).

10. "Partai-Partai Politik Indonesia: Ideologi, Strategi dan Program 2004–2009", *Kompas*, February 2004, p. 174.

11. Partai-Partai Politik 2004–2009, p. 305.

12. *Jakarta Post* (2004*a*) and *Kompas* (2004*c*).

13. Apart from the twenty-two complaints filed by political parties and one by an alliance of political parties, the rest were by individual candidates for the Regional Representative Council (DPD) from across the country.

14. *Jakarta Post* (22 June 2004) reported that the constitutional court had completed the hearings on the electoral disputes. The court handed down 38 decisions on a number of disputes arising out of the 5 April 2004 election. The decision affected the number of seats of political parties in the House of Representatives and a number of provincial and regental legislatures.

15. *Jakarta Post* (2004*b*).

16. Endin Sofihara is for the speaker's post, and E.E. Mangindaan from the Democratic Party, Ahmad Farhan Hamid of the National Mandate Party (PAN) and Ali Masykur Musa (PKB) as his deputies (Taufiqurrahman 2004).

17. DPD members are grouped into three: West (10 provinces in Sumatra), Central (11 provinces in Java, Bali and Kalimantan) and East (11 provinces located in Irian Jaya, Sulawesi, and Irian Jaya).

18. Three rounds had to be conducted to elect the DPD speaker. Six candidates competed in the first round and this resulted in 49 votes for Ginandjar Kartasasmita from West Java, 29 votes for Irman Gusman from West Sumatra, 22 votes for Sarwono Kusumaatmadja from Jakarta, 18 votes for La Ode Ida from Southeast Sulawesi, 2 votes for Harun Al Rasyid from West Nusa Tenggara, 1 vote for Muhammad Natsir from Jambi and 1 vote for Kasmir Tri Putra from Lampung. Five votes were invalid and one vote abstained. Harun Al Rasyid, Muhammad Natsir, Kasmir Tri Putra and La Ode Ida decided to not join the second race. From the second round election of the DPD speaker, Ginandjar gained 59, Irman gained 43, and Sarwono gained 26, of the 128 votes. The run-off was unavoidable as none secured 50 per cent plus one (*Kompas*, 1 October 2004). "Ginandjar Kartasasmita Ketua DPD" and Swaranet "Ginandjar Kartasamita Akhirnya Raih Posisi Ketua DPD" <http://www.swara.tv/id/view_headline.php?ID=3412)>.

2

Political Parties at the Provincial Level
A Colourful Landscape

As discussed in the previous chapter, at the national level the six largest parties in the 1999 election survived in the 2004 parliamentary elections. However, in 2004, two of them, the PAN and PBB, dropped to seventh and eight positions respectively although these two parties still showed their importance at some provinces. Nevertheless, what happened at the national level may not necessarily reflect what occurred at the provincial level and therefore an examination at the provincial level is crucial. Discussions at the regional level provide a better picture of the colourful Indonesian political landscape, especially after the implementation of regional autonomy since 2001, which has greatly enhanced the power of the districts. However, this chapter limits the discussion to the support given by parties at the provincial level for the DPR and its trend in the last five years.

One of the consequences of the euphoria of the emerging democracy has been the rising desire to form special identities, based on ethnicity, religion, or economic considerations. Many districts and provinces have been splitting. Through *pemekaran*, or administrative fragmentation, Indonesia is getting carved up into more and more units (districts or provinces). In the 1999 election, Indonesia was divided into twenty-seven provinces, including East Timor which shortly became independent, and in the 2004 elections, Indonesia had grown to thirty-two provinces.[1] Each of six old provinces was split into two. South

Sumatra was split into South Sumatra and Bangka-Belitung, Riau into Riau and Riau Archipelago, West Java into West Java and Banten, North Sulawesi into North Sulawesi and Gorontalo, Maluku into Maluku and North Maluku, and Papua into Papua and West Irian Jaya.

This chapter begins with, and limits discussion to, who won and lost in the provinces, focusing on the six surviving old parties (Golkar, the PDI-P, PKB, PPP, PAN and PBB), followed by the emerging medium parties (the PD and PKS) and the four small parties (PBR, PDS, PKPB and PKPI). Figure 2.1 presents the political party landscape, representing where a party won the first place in the provinces, in 1999; while Figure 2.2 shows its change and continuity in 2004.

The description on each party is referred to in Chapter 1, while more detailed information on the votes gained by each of the twenty-four parties at the provincial level is presented in Appendix 3. To compare with the 2004 data, the 1999 provincial categorization was regrouped to follow the 2004 grouping with thirty-two provinces. The regrouping was based on the data at the districts belonging to the respective provinces. For example, the province of Riau Archipelago did not exist during the 1999 election. Therefore, the data for "this province" in 1999 was calculated by summing up the votes from the regency of Riau Islands and the city of Batam.[2]

Six Surviving Old Parties

Golkar (Golongan Karya)

Golkar took over the place of the PDI-P in the April election. As shown in Figure 2.2, Golkar finished first in twenty-six out of thirty-two provinces and it lost to other parties in six provinces, namely, Bangka-Belitung, Jakarta, Central Java, Yogyakarta, East Java and Bali. However, as shown in Figure 2.3, Golkar experienced declining support in many provinces in the last five years. More precisely, Golkar suffered from declining support in all provinces in Kalimantan and eastern Indonesia, but Golkar gained increasing support in Bali and some provinces in Java and Sumatra.

Golkar lost support in Sulawesi, perceived to be its stronghold, in eastern Indonesia. It suffered the most in Southeast Sulawesi, a poor province, with a decline of more than a quarter, from 63.1 per cent of the votes in 1999 to 36.8 per cent in 2004. It also lost its support in Central Sulawesi, where the communal tensions and mutual suspicion, particularly between Muslims and Christians, remain potential.

FIGURE 2.1
The Winning Parties in 1999

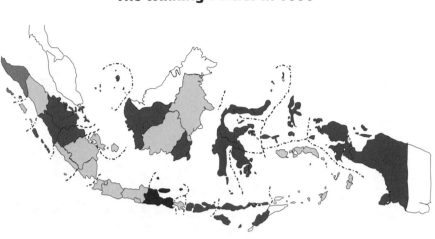

■Golkar □PDP ■PPP ■PKB

FIGURE 2.2
The Winning Parties in 2004

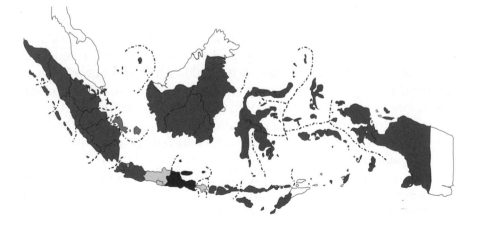

■ Golkar □ PDI-P ■ PBB ■ PKB □ PKS

FIGURE 2.3
Percentage of Golkar's Votes by Province:
Indonesia, 1999 and 2004

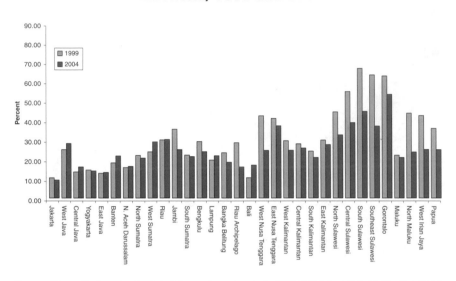

Source: Compiled and calculated from Ananta et al. (2004) Table 6.2.1, Table 7.4, Table 7.30 and Appendix 3.2.

Among all provinces in Indonesia, Gorontalo, the home province of Wiranto's wife, gained the largest percentage of support for Golkar. Despite the highest achievement in Gorontalo, the support for Golkar in this province had also declined from 62.5 per cent in 1999 to 53.1 per cent in 2004. Gorontalo[3] is a new province, a split based on religious composition from North Sulawesi and separated in 2000. It is an exclusively Muslim province, where Muslims constituted 98.2 per cent of the local population in 2000, while the "new" North Sulawesi is, in contrast, a province with non-Muslims constituting about 70 per cent of the population (Suryadinata, Arifin and Ananta 2003). In North Sulawesi, Golkar was not as strong as in Gorontalo; it only gained less than 30 per cent of the votes in 2004 but finished as the first winning party.

South Sulawesi, the home province of Golkar's top leaders such as former President B.J. Habibie and current Vice President Jusuf Kalla, is the province with the second largest support for Golkar. This province had the largest percentage of Golkar support in 1999, but Gorontalo's split from North Sulawesi had resulted in South Sulawesi attaining the second position in 2004. Nevertheless, the support for Golkar in South

Sulawesi, its largest stronghold, fell drastically from 66.5 per cent in 1999 to 44.3 per cent in 2004.

Therefore, despite its victory, there was a sign of rejection of Golkar in all the provinces in Sulawesi. The performance of some medium parties such as PD and PKS and a small party such as PDS and even two Golkar splits such as the PKPI and PKPB may have contributed to the decline in support for Golkar in Sulawesi. The discussion on these parties is in sub-sections of this chapter.

However, Golkar improved its performance in Java and Bali. Compared to the 1999 results, as shown in Figure 2.3, it obtained more votes in West Java, Central Java, East Java, Banten and Bali. Because of this good performance, the 2004 election results showed that Golkar constituents were no longer dominated by those residing in the Outer Islands. The majority of its constituents were from Java, constituting 52.8 per cent of the total vote for Golkar. In other words, five in ten Golkar constituents were more likely to be from Java. To be more specific, two in ten Golkar constituents were more likely to be from West Java. The share of West Java to Golkar constituents increased from 20.2 per cent in 1999 to 23.6 per cent in 2004. The 2004 result has contradicted the perception of Golkar's constituency as an Outer Islands party. In 1999, 53.3 per cent of the Golkar votes came from the Outer Islands (Ananta, Arifin and Suryadinata 2004).

Except in Bangka-Belitung, Golkar defeated other parties in other provinces of Sumatra in the 2004 elections. Golkar showed improvement in its gains in Lampung and West Sumatra between 1999 and 2004, and remained the same in Nanggroe Aceh Darussalam, Riau and South Sumatra. Because of poor performance of the PPP in Nanggroe Aceh Darussalam, the same gains for Golkar in the last five years made this party the winner in this province. Therefore, the PPP no longer controlled the power in any of the provinces in 2004. This indicates the weakening strength of the New Order Islamic-based party in the country.

Despite more than half of the Golkar votes being from Java, the seats for this party in the parliament were, interestingly, still dominated by the Outer Islands representatives, comprising 55.5 per cent of the total seats. South Sulawesi contributed around 20 per cent of the Outer Islands seats. As presented in Table 2.1, Golkar was the only party which had representatives from each of the thirty-two provinces, implying that Golkar's power had penetrated all provinces.

Finally, in most provinces, Golkar did not obtain better support than that in 1999. Golkar's victory in 2004 was because of the drastic

TABLE 2.1
Seats Allocation by Party and Province: Results of the Parliamentary Election

Province	GOLKAR	PDI-P	PPP	PD	PAN	PKB	PKS	PBR	PDS	PBB	PDK	PP	PKPB	PKPI	PPDI	PNI	TOTAL #	%
Jakarta	2	3	2	5	2	–	5	–	2	–	–	–	–	–	–	–	21	3.82
West Java	24	18	13	9	8	3	13	–	1	1	–	–	–	–	–	–	90	16.36
Central Java	12	24	8	8	8	13	3	–	–	1	–	–	–	–	–	–	76	13.82
Yogyakarta	1	2	–	1	2	1	1	–	–	–	–	–	–	–	–	–	8	1.45
East Java	13	20	8	9	6	28	2	1	–	1	–	–	–	–	–	–	86	15.64
Banten	5	4	2	2	2	2	3	2	–	1	–	–	–	–	–	–	22	4.00
Aceh	2	0	2	2	2	–	2	2	–	1	–	1	–	–	–	–	13	2.36
North Sumatra	6	5	3	3	3	–	2	3	3	–	–	1	–	–	–	–	29	5.27
West Sumatra	4	0	2	1	2	–	2	1	–	2	–	–	–	–	–	–	14	2.55
Riau	3	1	1	1	1	1	1	1	–	1	–	–	–	–	–	–	11	2.00
Jambi	2	1	1	1	1	–	1	–	–	–	–	–	–	–	–	–	7	1.27
South Sumatra	4	2	2	2	2	1	1	1	–	1	–	–	–	–	–	–	16	2.91
Bengkulu	1	1	1	–	1	–	–	–	–	–	–	–	–	–	–	–	4	0.73
Lampung	4	4	1	2	2	1	2	–	–	–	–	–	1	–	–	–	17	3.09
Bangka Belitung	1	1	–	–	–	–	–	–	–	1	–	–	–	–	–	–	3	0.55
Riau Archipelago	1	1	–	–	1	–	–	–	–	–	–	–	–	–	–	–	3	0.55
Bali	2	5	–	1	–	–	–	–	–	–	–	–	1	–	–	–	9	1.64
West Nusa Tenggara	3	1	1	1	1	–	1	1	–	–	–	–	–	1	–	–	10	1.82
East Nusa Tenggara	5	3	–	1	–	–	–	–	1	–	–	1	–	1	1	–	13	2.36

																	Total	%
West Kalimantan	3	2	1	1	1	–	1	1	–	–	–	–	–	–	–	–	10	1.82
Central Kalimantan	2	1	1	1	1	–	–	–	–	–	–	–	–	–	–	–	6	1.09
South Kalimantan	2	1	2	1	1	1	1	1	–	–	1	–	–	–	–	–	11	2.00
East Kalimantan	2	1	1	1	1	–	1	–	–	–	–	–	–	–	–	–	7	1.27
North Sulawesi	2	1	1	–	–	–	–	1	1	–	–	–	–	–	–	–	6	1.09
Central Sulawesi	2	1	1	1	–	–	1	–	–	–	–	–	–	–	–	–	6	1.09
South Sulawesi	10	2	2	2	2	–	2	–	–	2	2	–	–	–	–	–	24	4.36
Southeast Sulawesi	2	1	1	1	–	–	–	–	–	–	–	–	–	–	–	–	5	0.91
Gorontalo	2	–	–	–	–	–	–	–	–	1	–	–	–	–	–	–	3	0.55
Maluku	1	1	–	1	–	–	1	–	–	–	–	–	–	–	–	–	4	0.73
North Maluku	1	–	–	1	–	–	1	–	–	–	–	–	–	–	–	–	3	0.55
West Irian Jaya	1	1	–	–	–	–	–	–	1	–	–	–	–	–	–	–	3	0.55
Papua	3	1	–	1	1	1	–	–	–	1	–	1	–	1	–	–	10	1.82
NATIONAL	128	109	58	55	53	52	45	14	13	11	4	3	2	1	1	1	550	100.00
Percentage	23.27	19.82	10.55	10.00	9.64	9.45	8.18	2.55	2.36	2.00	0.73	0.55	0.36	0.18	0.18	0.18	100	

Source: Compiled from <www.kpu.go.id>.

drop in the PDI-P's popularity, which was the first winner in 1999 — thus, the victory does not imply that Golkar obtained more support in 2004 than in 1999 (see the analysis on the PDI-P performance in the following sub-section).

PDI-P (*Partai Demokrasi Indonesia — Perjuangan*)

The PDI-P, the Indonesian Democratic Party of Struggle, which was the winning party in 1999 securing 33.8 per cent of the votes, suffered a massive decline and only managed to obtain 18.5 per cent of the votes in the 2004 election. The unhappiness and dissatisfaction of the PDI-P constituents were clearly shown by the poor performance of the party in all thirty-two provinces as presented in Figure 2.4. In most cases, its votes dropped by more than 10.0 per cent between 1999 and 2004.

The PDI-P secured first position only in three provinces, namely, Yogyakarta, Central Java, and Bali. Bali was still the same as in 1999, the greatest victory for Megawati's party. However, this party only secured 52.5 per cent of the votes in Bali, a big drop from 79.0 per cent in 1999. This might be partly because of the disenchantment with the

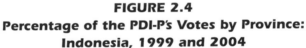

FIGURE 2.4
Percentage of the PDI-P's Votes by Province:
Indonesia, 1999 and 2004

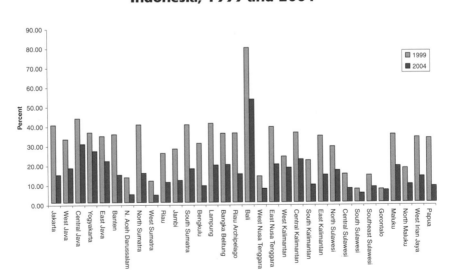

Source: Compiled and calculated from Ananta et al. (2004) Table 6.2.1, Table 7.4, Table 7.30 and Appendix 3.2.

then President Megawati, the chairperson of the PDI-P, especially after the Bali bombing on 12 October 2002, which put Indonesia and other countries in a state of shock. It devastated the Balinese emotionally and economically. In Central Java, this party only secured about 30.0 per cent of the votes, a drop from 42.8 per cent in 1999, and in Yogyakarta the party gained 26.2 per cent, a decline from 35.7 per cent in 1999. These three provinces had always been the strongholds of the PDI and later PDI-P, with Bali as the home of the Balinese and Central Java and Yogyakarta as the homes of the Javanese. The falling support from these provinces showed that Megawati was in trouble. This would have an important impact on her overall chance to be re-elected as the president in the first direct presidential elections. Yudhoyono, one of her main contenders, is also Javanese whose popularity was skyrocketing through the PD, a new party.

In 2004 the PDI-P also lost to Golkar in Central Kalimantan, East Kalimantan, and Maluku as well as in two provinces in the island of Java (West Java and Banten). In East Kalimantan, the PDI-P loss would probably be related to Megawati's seemingly indifference to the fate of the hundreds of thousands of illegal migrant workers who fled from Sabah, Malaysia, and formed "refugee camps" in the border town of Nunukan, East Kalimantan, in 2002 to avoid a crackdown from the government of Malaysia. This "Nunukan Tragedy" was a serious blow to the Megawati administration.[4]

Central Kalimantan had a different problem. People in this province might not have been happy with the way the government had managed communal conflicts, based on ethnic groups, between Madura and Dayak. The prolonged communal conflicts along religious lines in Maluku might have caused the dissatisfaction towards the government, and therefore the PDI-P. The unhappiness towards the PDI-P in Maluku, where the number of Muslims and non-Muslims were almost equal, was partly reflected in the support for the PDS, a party with Christians as its main constituents. The rise of support for the Javanese-based PKB, which was increasingly active in capturing non-Muslim votes, may have also contributed to the decline in support for the Javanese-based PDI-P in Maluku (see more discussions on these two parties in the later section of this chapter).

The Javanese-based PDI-P had become much less popular in West Sumatra, where the Javanese constituted only about 4.5 per cent of the population, the lowest concentration in Sumatra. This party only garnered 3.7 per cent of the votes, the lowest percentage among provinces in 2004 and a drop from 10.9 per cent of the votes in 1999.

Many of those who voted for the PDI-P in 1999 may have switched to the PKS, PD or Golkar in 2004.

As in the previous election, the PDI-P's constituents came mostly from Java constituting 71.2 per cent of the PDI-P voters in 2004. It was an increase from 67.9 per cent in 1999. In other words, the PDI-P's constituents were more Java-based. The largest number of its constituents was from Central Java, the PDI-P's traditional stronghold, where its share increased from 20.8 per cent in 1999 to 25.0 per cent in 2004. The second largest came from East Java (20.6 per cent) and then West Java (17.2 per cent).

Unlike Golkar, the PDI-P did not have representatives from all provinces in the parliament. The PDI-P did not get any representative from four provinces with Muslims constituting large percentages of the population, namely, Nanggroe Aceh Darussalam, West Sumatra, Gorontalo and North Maluku — all of which were located in the Outer Islands. In the first three provinces, the population comprised almost exclusively Muslims, with percentages larger than 97.5 per cent of the 2000 population. Meanwhile, North Maluku had 85.0 per cent of its population as Muslims (Suryadinata, Arifin and Ananta 2003). The Muslims in these provinces might have perceived that the PDI-P could not represent their Islamic aspirations.

Furthermore, the PDI-P seats in parliament had become much more a party of its heartland in Java comprising 65.1 per cent of its members of parliament coming from Java, or 71 seats out of 109 seats, indicating that the PDI-P had become more Java-centred. Therefore, the PDI-P could still be considered as a Java-based party. Another party perceived in the same way is the PKB, Gus Dur's party, discussed in the following section.

PKB (*Partai Kebangkitan Bangsa*)

The political outlook of the PKB, the National Awakening Party, cannot be separated from that of Gus Dur, co-founder of the party, a former president and also former chairman of the country's largest Muslim organization, the Nahdlatul Ulama (NU). The party was established by Gus Dur's grandfather Hasyim Asy'ari, and is inseparable from the NU, because most of its members also hail from the NU. At the national level, this party gained 10.6 per cent of the votes in 2004 and remained third in the post-authoritarian regime elections. At the provincial level, East Java, the strong base of the PKB with many NU members residing there and where Gus Dur has his residence, was the only province where the PKB secured first place in the last five years. However, the strength of this party in this province seems to have been weakening in recent years. The percentage of votes gained by this party declined from 35.5 per cent in 1999 to 30.6 per cent in 2004. This could possibly be attributed to the emerging popularity of the PKS and also the presence of the new Democrat Party. In fact, Yudhoyono was born in Pacitan, East Java and his mother is now residing in another city there, Blitar. The gain for these two emerging parties combined was quite significant at about 10.6 per cent. Golkar in East Java remained at about 13.0 per cent, as the third party. The PKB and PDI-P were the largest two parties in East Java, suffering from declining support in the last five years. On the other hand, the smallest support (1.3 per cent) for the PKB in 2004 appeared to be in North Maluku. As in 1999, the PKB there was not really getting more popular, as its gain remained the same.

The PKB has a reputation among non-Muslim and minority groups as an inclusive and tolerant political party. Even though the PKB historically belongs to the Nahdlatul Ulama (NU), the party's commitment in upholding democracy and openness is honoured by non-Muslims across the country especially for part of eastern Indonesia. Gus Dur said in the fifth anniversary celebration of this party in Central Java that "Christian prominent people, like Priest Erari in Jayapura and traditional leaders in Papua, told me some days ago of their readiness to give the votes of their followers to the PKB, so that the vote's percentage of the party in the province could be more than in East Java in the next 2004 election."[5]

During Gus Dur's presidency, the PKB made significant investments in inter-religious relations and minority rights protection efforts. The party's communal and inclusive stance has also extended not only to the ethnic Chinese community but also to other minority groups. North Sumatra, North Sulawesi, Maluku, Papua, West Irian Jaya, East Nusa Tenggara and West Kalimantan, where there were relatively large percentages of non-Muslims, were considered all fertile soil for the PKB.

However, before the April election, it was not clear whether the PKB's reputation as a pluralistic party would remain. The results of the April 2004 general election provide an opportunity to assess this question. The performance of the PKB in each province from 1999 to 2004 is presented in Figure 2.5. It shows that during that period the percentage of the votes for the PKB declined in all provinces in Java and Bali, except in Jakarta which remained the same. In most cases in Sumatra, the percentage of the votes gained by this party increased except in South Sumatra and Lampung.

FIGURE 2.5
Percentage of PKB's Votes by Province:
Indonesia, 1999 and 2004

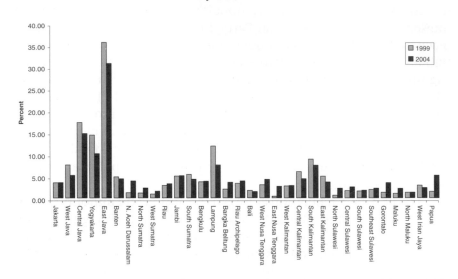

Source: Compiled and calculated from Ananta et al. (2004) Table 6.2.1, Table 7.4, Table 7.30 and Appendix 3.2.

On the other hand, the PKB seemed to have been able to obtain some support from the Christian community, especially in the Outer Islands. The PKB might have moved towards a more open and pluralistic party. The largest increase of support, from 1.5 per cent in 1999 to 5.1 per cent in 2004, was found in Papua, where Christians formed 75.5 per cent of the population in the province in 2000. In another Protestant-based province of North Sumatra, which is managed by the Batak Protestant Parish (HKBP), the PKB had made a unique effort to recruit the Christians. It had some HKBP figures in charge at provincial and districts levels, either in executive or supervisory boards. As a result, the votes gained by the PKB were doubled, from 1.1 per cent in 1999 to 2.3 per cent in 2004. The rising vote for this party was even bigger in North Sulawesi, another Christian province. It increased from 0.6 per cent in 1999 to 2.2 per cent in 2004. In short, as seen in Figure 2.5, the votes for the PKB in all provinces with large percentages of non-Muslims increased tremendously.

Despite its increasing popularity in the Outer Islands, the PKB dominance in Java declined. They accounted for 87.5 per cent of the total PKB voters in 2004, a decline from 90.3 per cent in 1999. As in

1999, the PKB constituents resided predominantly in East Java, with 52.5 per cent of the total PKB voters, followed by those who resided in Central Java, 21.5 per cent. In other words, the PKB is still rooted too exclusively in a single province and more precisely, a single segment of society, because of the fact that the PKB membership traditionally derives from the NU, mostly from rural Java, particularly East Java. Furthermore, in the parliament, most seats of this party also represented Java with only five seats from the Outer Islands, namely Riau, South Sumatra, Lampung, Central Kalimantan and Papua. Therefore, this party is still heavily Java and Javanese-centred, even though the 2004 elections have shown that the weight of Java and Javanese has somewhat declined.

PPP (Partai Persatuan Pembangunan)

Like the PKB, the PPP, the United Development Party (the old Islamic party), remained in the same position at the national level — it was also fourth in the 2004 elections. In 1999, the PPP was the leading party in one province only, Nanggroe Aceh Darussalam, but it lost to Golkar in April 2004, and had taken second position. Furthermore, as in the 1999 election, the PPP did not win the first position in any other province in this election.

Across provinces, the votes ranged from as high as 14.2 per cent in South Kalimantan to as low as 0.9 per cent in Bali. Figure 2.6 shows the trends of the PPP gain in each province in 1999 and 2004. It shows that the party only managed to strengthen its constituents in four provinces (Bengkulu, East Java, Southeast Sulawesi and West Irian Jaya), remained the same in Yogyakarta and Bali, but it obtained fewer votes in the remaining provinces. For example, in Nanggroe Aceh Darussalam, its votes declined by more than half from 28.8 per cent in 1999 to 13.8 per cent in 2004. It is perhaps partly because of the emergence of its rival party, the PBR, lead by Zainuddin M.Z. As a new party contesting for the first time in the election, the PBR in this province performed quite well by securing 7.4 per cent of the votes and finishing as the fifth party after Golkar, PAN, PPP, and PKS. The PKS could also be another factor in the declining performance of the PPP there. It gained a great increase in this province, from 1.6 per cent in 1999 to 9.1 per cent in 2004.

As seen in Figure 2.6, other big losses for this party were in Maluku and North Maluku. This could be because of the emerging popularity of the PBR and PKS. In both provinces the PBR gained about half of the PPP votes. In Maluku, the PKS doubled the votes in the last five years

FIGURE 2.6
Percentage of the PPP's Votes by Province:
Indonesia, 1999 and 2004

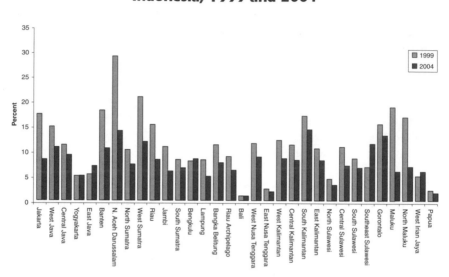

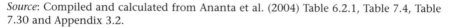

Source: Compiled and calculated from Ananta et al. (2004) Table 6.2.1, Table 7.4, Table 7.30 and Appendix 3.2.

and took the third position. Moreover, in North Maluku the party gained more than seven times that in the previous election. More precisely, the PKS gained 1.5 per cent of the votes in 1999 and 10.6 per cent in 2004. There, the PKS controlled the power as the second largest party.

As the other three parties mentioned earlier, the voters for the PPP also mostly resided in Java with about 66.2 per cent, consisting of 23.7 per cent in West Java, 17.2 per cent in Central Java, 15.2 per cent in East Java and the rest in the remaining provinces in Java. Meanwhile, in parliament, Java was represented by 56.9 per cent of the PPP's seats. This composition may simply represent the ratio of the population in Java and the Outer Islands, and hence it is difficult to say whether the Outer Islands voters were more likely to vote for the PPP — it may no longer be the party of the Outer Islands.

PAN (*Partai Amanat Nasional*)
At the national level, PAN, the National Mandate Party, gained slightly less than it did in the 1999 election, a decline from 7.0 per cent in 1999 to 6.4 per cent in 2004. This unfavourable performance of PAN may be

closely related to the declining popularity of Amien Rais, the chairman of PAN, as a presidential candidate.[6] Amien's indecisiveness on whether to portray PAN and himself as either pluralistic or Islamic may have resulted in some voters choosing another party, which more clearly showed their orientation — either pluralistic or Islamic. Some of the PAN 1999 voters might have chosen the PBB or PKS, as these two Islamic parties competed for similar sources of support, in particular the Muhammadiyah.

PAN lost severely in Jakarta, from 16.8 per cent in 1999 to 7.0 per cent in 2004, mainly because of the rise of the PKS, which secured the first place in Jakarta, with 22.3 per cent of the votes. The rise of the PD, the second winner in Jakarta, may have also taken some of the PAN urban educated supporters. PAN also gained less support in Nanggroe Aceh Darussalam, dropping from 17.8 per cent in 1999 to 13.3 per cent in 2004, particularly because of the rise of the PKS.

As in 1999, PAN did not emerge as the winner in any province in 2004. At most, it secured the second in the same provinces as in 1999: West Sumatra (22.2 per cent in 1999 and 14.2 per cent in 2004), Yogyakarta (17.3 per cent in 1999 and 17.8 per cent in 2004), and Jambi (6.7 per cent in 1999 and 17.6 per cent in 2004). However, among these three provinces, only in Jambi did PAN gain a stronger position; in Yogyakarta, it remained the same and in West Sumatra, it saw declining support.

Nanggroe Aceh Darussalam and Riau Archipelago were two other provinces securing more than 10 per cent of the votes for PAN in 2004. It was not surprising that this party gained good support in Nanggroe Aceh Darussalam, though Golkar was the winner. Its population was predominantly Muslim but their support was divided into other Islamic parties such as the PPP, the second winner, and the PKS, the fourth. The combined votes for the PPP, PAN and PKS constituted 36.3 per cent of the total vote in this province.

In Riau Archipelago, the first two largest parties were Golkar and the PDI-P, reflecting the old party and pluralistic preferences. The next two largest parties were the PKS and PAN, reflecting the more educated, urban, and Islamic preferences. Riau Archipelago is a migrant province, with a relatively more educated population.

However, Figure 2.7 indicates that there were more provinces where the PAN gained a larger number of votes than where it lost. Nearly all provinces in eastern Indonesia showed that the PAN gained more votes in 2004. In Papua, a province with a large percentage of Christians, this party gained one seat in the parliament. Just like the PKB, as shown

FIGURE 2.7
Percentage of PAN's Votes by Province:
Indonesia, 1999 and 2004

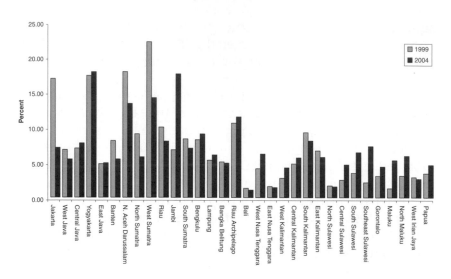

Source: Compiled and calculated from Ananta et al. (2004) Table 6.2.1, Table 7.4, Table 7.30 and Appendix 3.2.

in Figure 2.7, the PAN has also built a reputation among non-Muslim and small ethnic groups.

In terms of geographical distribution, 60.1 per cent of the PAN voters resided in Java, with 18.5 per cent residing in Central Java, 15.3 per cent in West Java, 13.7 per cent in East Java and the rest in the remaining provinces of the island. In the parliament, 28 out of 53 seats were from Java. This composition may simply show the ratio of the voters in Java and the Outer Islands, and hence the PAN may be considered as a party of voters in both Java and the Outer Islands.

PBB (*Partai Bulan Bintang*)

The PBB, the Crescent Star Party, had expected that more Muslim voters would have chosen the party instead of secular nationalist parties such as the PDI-P, Golkar, and PD, as well as the increasingly secular Muslim-based parties, like the PKB and PAN. Yet, the PBB again received less than 3.0 per cent of the votes at the national level in 2004, though its performance in 2004 was better than in 1999. It is the only old surviving party that was able to have an increase, though very modest, in the percentage of its support. It also showed improvements in all provinces. In 2004 it repeated its success in Bangka-Belitung, the home province of the party chairman, Yusril Ihza Mahendra, with the highest percentage of votes for the PBB among all thirty-two provinces in Indonesia. Furthermore, the PBB secured the first winner in Bangka-Belitung in 2004, and this was the only province where it finished first in these elections. From this province, the PBB had one of eleven seats in parliament.

The second largest percentage of the votes for this party in 2004 was West Nusa Tenggara. As shown in Figure 2.8 it was a dramatic increase from what they had in 1999. As shown in Figure 2.8, the votes for the PBB in the eastern Indonesian provinces mostly increased significantly between 1999 and 2004. These provinces secured only less than 4 per cent of the votes in 1999, but had gained nearly 7.0 per cent in 2004.

Unlike the five parties mentioned earlier, 55.0 per cent of the PBB voters were scattered in the Outer Islands. West Java, as one of the most populous provinces, was where around one-fifth of the PBB voters were. In the parliament, only two seats were gained from Java and these came from West Java and Banten.

FIGURE 2.8
Percentage of PBB's Votes by Province:
Indonesia, 1999 and 2004

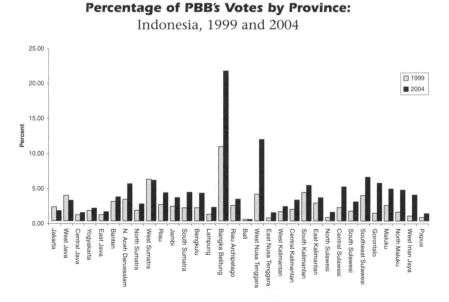

Source: Compiled and calculated from Ananta et al. (2004) Table 6.2.1, Table 7.4, Table 7.30 and Appendix 3.2.

The PBB remains as a small Islamic party. The rise of the PKS, an Islamic party which had emerged as a new star in 2004, may have occurred at the expense of the PBB. Doni (2004) mentioned that the PKS used a very different strategy from the one used by the PBB to woo the Muslims, especially the Muhammadiyah. The PKS strove, for example, to show that "being Islamic" was being clean, peaceful, and orderly. On the other hand, the PBB tried to incorporate Islamic doctrines in the drafting of the criminal code, including sexual behaviour. This attempt was strongly opposed by both Muslim and non-Muslim groups. Therefore, it was not surprising that the PKS took over the PBB's strong areas such as Jakarta, where the PBB gained a significant number of votes in 1999. There, the PKS managed to be a dominant party in the April 2004 election, indicating that the party had been able to sway the PBB voters (see the discussion on the PKS in the following section).

Emerging Medium Parties

PD (Partai Demokrat)
The PD, Democrat Party, is a new party, closely associated with Yudhoyono. With the history of the establishment of the party, as discussed in Chapter 1, the PD is often seen as the party for those who were disappointed with the old *Pancasila* parties — Golkar, and particularly, the PDI-P. Therefore, the success of the PD may have been at the expense of Golkar and the PDI-P.

The rapidly rising popularity of Yudhoyono brought this party to the fifth position at the national level, grabbing 7.5 per cent of the vote, or 8.5 million votes.[7] Though the party's achievement varied across provinces, votes gained by this party in all provinces were above 3 per cent, except in Gorontalo, where it lost to Golkar and only managed to gain 0.9 per cent of the votes (see Figure 2.9, which also indicates the successful performance of the PD in Jakarta, North Sulawesi, and South Sumatra).

In Jakarta, the party managed to be the second winner of the election securing 20.2 per cent of the vote, slightly behind the PKS, but far ahead of the two old "big" parties, the PDI-P and Golkar. From Jakarta, this party gained five seats, or almost 10 per cent of the total seats in the parliament. The importance in Jakarta of the PD, a party with a pluralistic orientation, might have revealed the rejection of the people towards the two major old pluralistic parties, Golkar and the PDI-P. The more urban-orientation of the PD might have been another magnet for the voters in the capital of Indonesia.

FIGURE 2.9
Percentage and Number of PD's Votes by Province:
Indonesia, 2004

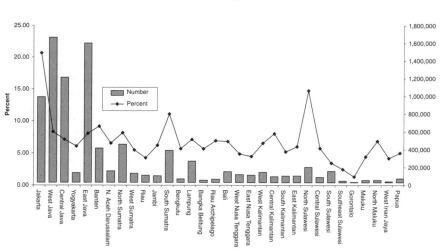

Source: Compiled and calculated from Appendix 3.2.

In the Outer Islands, the PD performed tremendously well in North Sulawesi with 14.3 per cent of the votes, placing them fourth after Golkar (32.3 per cent), the PDI-P (16.2 per cent) and PDS (14.8 per cent). These four *Pancasila* parties might have vied for the non-Muslims who constituted 70.5 per cent of the population in 2000 — altogether these four parties earned 77.6 per cent of the total vote in North Sulawesi. This phenomenon could also be an expression of the unhappiness towards Golkar and the PDI-P. The voters wanted to have something new. Some of them threw their support to the Christian-based PDS, while others supported the PD, Yudhoyono's party.

Among all provinces, the third largest gain by the PD was in South Sumatra, with 10.7 per cent. It obtained two seats from this province. At the expense of the PDI-P, the PD was the third largest party in South Sumatra despite the fact that Taufik Kemas, the husband of Megawati, came from here.

The votes for the PD were concentrated in Java, especially in West Java, Central Java, East Java and Jakarta. In the parliament, 61.8 per cent of the PD's seats were from Java, almost the same as the ratio of the voters in Java and the Outer Islands. The Java and the Outer Islands dichotomy may not work for this party.

PKS (*Partai Keadilan Sejahtera*)

The PKS, Prosperous Justice Party, known as the PK in the 1999 election securing only 1.4 per cent of the votes, won 7.3 per cent of the votes, or 8.2 per cent of the seats in the 2004 elections. This party secured the sixth place in April 2004 at the national level, ahead of PAN, the seventh.

However, in Jakarta where voting patterns are often considered the barometer of Indonesian politics, the PKS finished first, securing 22.3 per cent of the votes in 2004. It was a very large increase from 4.9 per cent in 1999. The dramatic rise of the Islamic PKS might have been at the expense of the old Islamic PPP and particularly the PAN, a *Pancasila* party with Muslims as their main constituents. The PPP's support in Jakarta declined drastically from 17.2 per cent in 1999 to 8.2 per cent in 2004, while that for PAN, from 16.9 per cent in 1999 to 7.0 per cent in 2004. Both the PKS and PAN competed for the Muhammadiyah, urban and educated Muslim, constituents. Some attempts by Amien Rais, the chairperson of PAN, to woo the non-Muslims, might have caused some of PAN's supporters to leave PAN and join the PKS.

The PKS together with the PD comprised 42.5 per cent of the votes in Jakarta. As seen in Figure 2.10, the PDI-P and Golkar were far behind

FIGURE 2.10
Composition of Votes for the National Parliament:
Jakarta, 2004

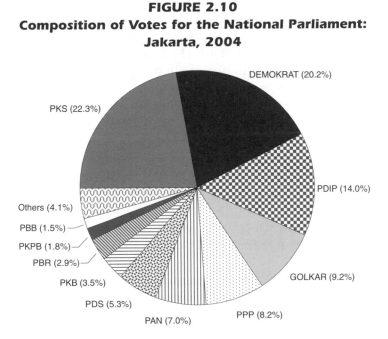

Source: Compiled and calculated from Appendix 3.2.

the PKS and PD. These two old parties only gained five seats altogether — three seats from the PDI-P and two seats from Golkar. The number of seats for Golkar was the same as those for the PPP, PAN and PDS. The Jakarta phenomenon may indicate a break from the continuing support of the old parties, perhaps reflecting the desire of Jakarta's voters for change.

Apart from Jakarta, there were six other provinces where the PKS won more than 10 per cent of the votes. As presented in Figure 2.11 these six provinces were: West Sumatra, Riau Archipelago, West Java, Banten, South Kalimantan and North Maluku. As expected, the Islamic PKS gained the smallest support, less than 2.0 per cent of the votes, in Bali, East Nusa Tenggara and North Sulawesi, where there was a large concentration of the non-Muslim population.

Four Small Parties

In this section only four small parties have been selected for discussion: those which gained more than 2.0 per cent of the votes and one party which supported Yudhoyono.

FIGURE 2.11
Percentage of PKS' Votes by Province:
Indonesia, 1999 and 2004

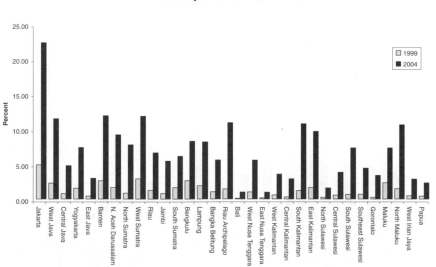

Source: Compiled and calculated from Ananta et al. (2004) Table 6.2.1, Table 7.4, Table 7.30 and Appendix 3.2.

PBR (*Partai Bintang Reformasi*)

The PBR, Reformed Star Party that split from the PPP and was led by a cleric, targetted to gain 3 per cent of the votes for its first contest in the elections, but only gained 2.4 per cent or 2.8 million votes. However, as shown in Figure 2.12, it gained above 2.4 per cent in some provinces in the Outer Islands. The highest gain by this party was in West Nusa Tenggara, at 7.9 per cent, followed by Nanggroe Aceh Darussalam. In Java, it mostly gained less than 2.0 per cent. In terms of the number of votes, it was distributed in all provinces ranging from about 391,000 in West Java to only about 2,000 in Bali. Voters from Java comprised around 40.5 per cent of the total PBR vote. In other words, nearly 60 per cent of voters resided in the Outer Islands. Yet, in terms of the number of seats, the PBR was almost exclusively the party of the Outer Islands — 13 out of 14 seats gained by this party in the parliament were from the Outer Islands. One seat in Java was from Banten, making the PBR a non-Java party.

PDS (*Partai Damai Sejahtera*)

As a party with Christians as its main constituents, reflected in its logo featuring a cross and a white pigeon, the PDS, Prosperous Peace Party, gained significant votes in Christian-dominant provinces like North

FIGURE 2.12
Percentage and Number of PBR's Votes by Province:
Indonesia, 2004

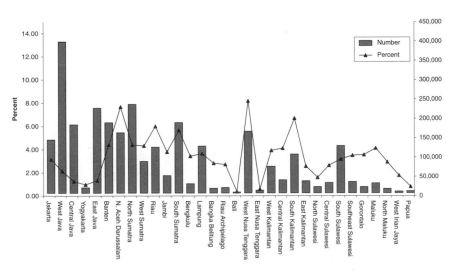

Source: Compiled and calculated from Appendix 3.2.

Sulawesi where it secured 14.8 per cent of the votes, the highest it won among the provinces (see Figure 2.13). The Christians formed 70.5 per cent of the population in this province in 2000. Yet, the majority of the Christians did not vote for the PDS, but were spread among Golkar, the PDI-P, and also the PD.

The PDS had a good showing in the very eastern provinces of Indonesia, as presented in Figure 2.13, where it gained between 5 per cent and 10 per cent of the votes. Communal violence is now quiet in Ambon (the capital city of Maluku) and North Maluku partly because they have been completely segregated administratively. However, the peace may remain fragile. In both provinces, polarization showed up in the April election results, with Christian communities likely to vote for the PDS and their Muslim neighbours likely to vote for the PKS. In Maluku, the percentage of votes for the PDS (8.6 per cent) was similar to that for the PKS (7.3 per cent). The emergence of these two parties might have been at the expense of Golkar and the PDI-P. The PDS in North Maluku secured more or less the same support as in Maluku, but the PKS gained more with 10.2 per cent of the votes, as the second winner after Golkar.

Outside eastern Indonesia, the PDS earned 6.1 per cent of the votes in North Sumatra, where 34.6 per cent of the population in 2000 were

FIGURE 2.13
Percentage and Number of PDS' Votes by Province: Indonesia, 2004

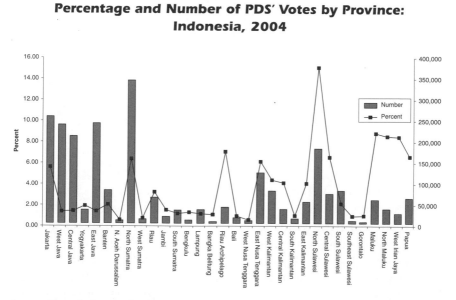

Source: Compiled and calculated from Appendix 3.2.

non-Muslims. The PDS was slightly behind the PKS. On the other hand, the PDS also obtained 6.8 per cent of the votes in the province of Riau Archipelago though the non-Muslims only comprised 17.7 per cent of the population. In Riau Archipelago, the PKS managed to secure 10.9 per cent of the votes. It is an interesting phenomenon that in some provinces the PKS and PDS received almost equal support from the population. Both are parties with a religious orientation but they do not overtly show their religious orientation in their campaigns and programmes. Both, for example, emphasized clean government.

In terms of absolute size of its constituents, the largest number of votes for the PDS came from North Sumatra, where many Christian Batak live, followed by Jakarta, East Java, West Java, Central Java and North Sulawesi. All these provinces gained more than 150,000 votes. However, the PDS only obtained seats from North Sumatra (3 seats), Jakarta (2 seats), West Java (1 seat) and North Sulawesi (1 seat). The PDS did not gain any seat from Central Java and East Java. Of interest to note is that the PDS voters who resided in Java comprised 43.1 per cent, almost half of its supporters, and much larger than the percentage of Christians living in Java. This may imply that the Christians in Java were more likely to vote for the PDS than the Christians in the Outer Islands. However, because of the more "expensive" seats in Java, the PDS representatives were mostly from the Outer Islands — ten out of thirteen seats.

From the seven Christian-based political parties which went through the registration process at the Justice and Human Rights Ministry for the 2004 elections, the PDS was the only one able to compete in the 2004 elections. As a Christian-based political party, its achievement was remarkable and significant compared to the 1999 election when the PDKB (Love the Nation Democratic Party) only managed five seats, and Krisna (Indonesian Christian National Party) and the PKD (Democratic Catholic Party) gained none.

PKPB (*Partai Karya Peduli Bangsa*)

Though it was a split from Golkar, the PKPB (Concern for the Nation Functional Party), led by Hartono, a retired general and close ally of one of Soeharto's daughters, itself did not represent any real threat to Golkar. It had little voter recognition as a "new Golkar" at both national and provincial levels, though it had played an important role in some districts. As a new party contesting for the first time in the elections, the PKPB showed considerable gain, garnering 2.1 per cent of the votes, or 2.4 million votes. Nearly 60.0 per cent of the

FIGURE 2.14
Percentage and Number of PKPB's Votes by Province:
Indonesia, 2004

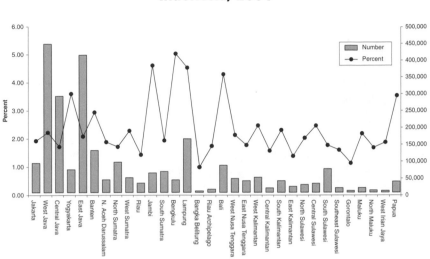

Source: Compiled and calculated from Appendix 3.2.

voters resided in Java, especially from the three populous provinces (West Java, Central Java and East Java). As shown in Figure 2.14, six provinces (Jambi, Bengkulu, Lampung, Yogyakarta, Bali and Papua) gained more than 3.0 per cent of the votes. However, the PKPB has only two seats in the parliament, one from Lampung and another from Bali.

PKPI (Partai Keadilan dan Persatuan Indonesia)
The PKPI (Indonesian Justice and Unity Party), a split from Golkar and led by Eddie Sudrajat, a retired general, managed to garner 1.3 per cent of the votes for the national parliament. This party joined the PD in nominating Yudhoyono–Kalla as the presidential-vice presidential candidates. The gains ranged from 0.1 per cent in Gorontalo to 4.6 per cent in Central Sulawesi. As presented in Figure 2.15, in the majority of the provinces, located in the Outer Islands, it gained above 1.3 per cent. Out of 1.4 million votes, about 40 per cent were from Java, mainly from West Java and East Java. In other words, the PKPI was more popular in the Outer Islands. Because of its small number, it gained only one seat, from East Nusa Tenggara, in the parliament.

FIGURE 2.15
Percentage and Number of PKPI's Votes by Province: Indonesia, 2004

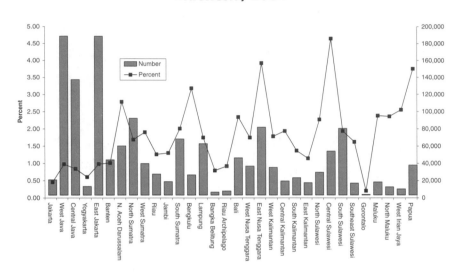

Source: Compiled and calculated from Appendix 3.2.

Concluding Remarks

Only four out of forty-eight parties competing in the 1999 election were in the top rankings at the provincial level. The PKB and PPP finished first only in one province. Nanggroe Aceh Darussalam was the only province the PPP won, while the PKB won first place in East Java only.

The PDI-P gained its victory in the 1999 election by dominating some populous provinces in Java such as West Java (including Banten) and Central Java, and some provinces in the southern part of Sumatra. Golkar occupied the remaining provinces, especially in eastern Indonesia. However, the Indonesian political party landscape has changed. The position of the PDI-P in some provinces was taken over by Golkar in the 2004 parliamentary election. In the Outer Islands, Golkar won in all provinces, except in Bali (PDI-P) and Bangka-Belitung (PBB). Bali is one of the strongholds of the PDI-P while Bangka-Belitung is the province where Yusril Ihza Mahendra, the PBB leader, comes from. This is also the first time and the only province that the PBB ever won the first place.

On the other hand, the political party landscape in Java is more colourful, as no party dominated the island and even a medium party was also able to win a number one position. Jakarta was for the PKS, Banten and West Java for Golkar, Yogyakarta and Central Java for the PDI-P, and East Java for the PKB. Gus Dur's ancestral home of East Java remained the PKB heartland. The PKS picked up more votes in Jakarta and secured the first position in 2004, defeating the 1999 winner, the PDI-P.

Though gaining victory, Golkar suffered a decline in the percentage of support in all provinces located in Kalimantan, Sulawesi, and other eastern provinces. Golkar increased the percentage of support in some provinces in western Indonesia. The constituents of Golkar also changed. In 1999, Golkar earned more votes in the Outer Islands, but in 2004, it gained more support in Java.

Compared to its performance in 1999, the PDI-P performed poorly in 2004. It retained its victory only in its three strongholds (Yogyakarta, Central Java, and Bali). Yet, the percentage of its support in these provinces also declined. Furthermore, in most provinces, the support declined by more than 10.0 per cent. Voters in provinces with relatively large percentages of Javanese and non-Muslims also shied away from the PDI-P.

The PKB kept its third position and its only stronghold, the province of East Java, though the percentage of support in this province also declined. Similarly, the PPP held the fourth position as it did in 1999. However, it lost Nanggroe Aceh Darussalam, its only victory in 1999, to Golkar. The rise of the PKS in this province may have helped in the victory of Golkar. The PPP did not win in any province and the majority of its voters lived in Java, especially West Java.

PAN suffered a drop in position from fifth in 1999 to seventh in 2004. As in 1999, it did not win in any province. However, in most provinces in eastern Indonesia, its performance in 2004 was slightly better than that in 1999. As with the other four parties, more voters lived in Java.

In short, this chapter has shown that though a general pattern of change in voting behaviour can been seen at the national level, an appreciation of the variations at the provinces is very important to obtain a better picture of electoral behaviour in Indonesia. Further studies should be done at the district (*kabupaten*) level, to enhance the understanding of Indonesia's colourful political landscape.

Notes

1.   The administrative fragmentation continues to grow. For example, South Sulawesi, as mentioned in *TEMPO Interaktif* dated 28 April 2001, is on the verge of falling into six provinces, because of people's dissatisfaction at the districts. They asked for five new provinces within South Sulawesi: Luwu Raya (Luwu and North Luwu), West Sulawesi (Majene, Polewali Mamasa and Mamuju), East Sulawesi (Bantaeng, Bulukumba, Sinjai and Selayar), Ajattapareng (Barru, Pangkajene Islands, Parepare, and Pinrang) and Bosowasi (Bone, Soppeng, Wajo and Sidenreng Rappang). The remaining six districts, Maros, Gowa, Takalar, Jeneponto, Tana Toraja and Makassar are to remain as South Sulawesi. However, only West Sulawesi was recently approved in 2004, not long before the then president Megawati left her presidential term, as the thirty-third province of Indonesia. It includes the regencies of Polewali Mandar, Mamasa, Majene, Mamuju, and North Mamuju. Mamasa is a split from Polewali Mamasa, and North Mamuju from Mamuju. Therefore, future studies at the provincial and district levels should pay attention to how *pemekaran* (administrative fragmentation) has grown.

2.   Later in October 1999, the regency of Riau Islands was expanded administratively by splitting into three regencies: Karimun, Natuna and Riau Islands. See Ananta, Arifin and Suryadinata (2004) for the number of votes gained by each of the seven parties at the district level.

3.   The Province of Gorontalo in 2004 consisted of four regencies, namely, Gorontalo, Boalemo, Pohuwato, and Bone Bolango, which was an expansion of the regency of Gorontalo and the city of Gorontalo. Therefore, Gorontalo is used to name the province, regency and city.

4.   For a more detailed discussion on the "Nunukan Tragedy", see Tirtosudarmo (2004).

5.   "Non-Muslims Grateful for PKB on Receptive Attitude", 25 August 2003. <http://www.gusdur.net>.

6.   See Chapter 3 for a discussion on the popularity of Amien Rais and other presidential candidates.

7.   See Chapter 3 for a discussion on the popularity of Yudhoyono and other presidential candidates.

3

No New President Yet
The First Contest

Soon after the parliamentary elections, Indonesia entered the first direct presidential elections. This chapter begins with a discussion on the individual popularity of candidates from December 2003 before they became the official presidential candidates. It is followed by a description of the five official pairs of these candidates. It then examines the popularity of the five pairs during the campaign period (June 2004) of the first round of the presidential elections and makes a comparison of what the pairs actually gained in the first round and what the pairs would have earned if voters had followed the lines of their supporting parties.

The Individual Popularity of Candidates

Prior to the first round of the presidential elections on 5 July 2004, there were several polling surveys on electoral preferences of the voters. However, to reduce error from comparisons among different methods and institutions, only the results from the International Foundation for Election Systems (IFES) are used here to assess the candidates' popularity from December 2003 until the first round of the presidential elections. Before the final five presidential candidates became official, there were more potential candidates as shown in Table 3.1. Therefore, surveys conducted by IFES did not limit the questions to the five candidates discussed in this chapter. It included eight others, namely

TABLE 3.1
Popularity of Presidential Candidates:
December 2003 – the First Round

Candidate	Dec	March	April	May	June	Late June	Election
Wiranto	3.0	3.3	2.2	10.0	11.4	14.2	22.2
Megawati	13.7	11.6	14.6	11.2	11.0	11.7	26.6
Amien	7.8	7.9	4.0	4.4	9.8	10.9	14.7
Yudhoyono	5.0	18.4	30.6	41.0	45.0	43.5	33.6
Hamzah	4.1	3.2	1.7	3.0	2.0	2.4	3.0
Yusril	5.5	3.7	2.2	1.8	*	*	*
Akbar	6.5	5.0	3.9	3.8	*	*	*
Sultan	3.0	0.3	*	*	*	*	*
Gus Dur	3.1	3.8	2.5	4.2	*	*	*
Hidayat N	1.3	1.7	4.1	3.9	*	*	*
Tutut	1.7	2.8	2.0	1.8	*	*	*
Zainuddin	4.3	2.4	*	*	*	*	*
Prabowo	*	2.9	4.8	*	*	*	*
Not Sure	26.8	26.4	21.0	14.0	20.8	17.4	*

Notes: Dec refers to survey on 13–18 December 2003
        March refers to survey on 21–28 March 2004
        April refers to survey on 7–14 April 2004
        May refers to survey on 1–8 May 2004
        June refers to survey on 4–9 June 2004
        Late June refers to survey on 17–26 June 2004
        Election refers to the official results of the first round of the elections
Source: IFES (2004*a*, 2004*b*, 2004*c*, 2004*d*, 2004*e*, 2004*f*).

Akbar Tanjung, Yusril Ihza Mahendra, Sultan Hamengkubuwono X, Siti Hardiyanti Rukmana (Tutut), Zainuddin MZ, Hidayat Nurwahid, Prabowo and Abdurrahman Wahid (Gus Dur).

In December 2003 the two retired generals — Wiranto and Yudhoyono — were not much favoured by the respondents. Wiranto was only preferred by 3 per cent of the respondents, while Yudhoyono, selected by 5 per cent of the respondents, was more popular than Wiranto. Akbar Tanjung and Yusril Ihza Mahendra, two civilians, were preferred to both Wiranto and Yudhoyono. Akbar was chosen by 6.5 per cent of the respondents and Yusril, by 5.5 per cent. On the other hand, two other civilian candidates, Megawati and Amien, were in the top positions to be the next president. The civilian candidates seemed to be more favoured than those with military backgrounds. This data indicated that in December 2003, people still knew very little about the two generals, or that they might not like candidates with military backgrounds. In fact, in November 2003, Yudhoyono was mainly discussed in the context of his possible vice-presidential candidacy to Megawati.[1]

However, by the end of March 2004, after resigning from the post of coordinating minister of politics and security affairs under Megawati's administration, and officially announcing his candidacy, Yudhoyono's popularity zoomed to leave Megawati and Amien behind. His more frequent appearances in the mass media might have helped in his rising popularity too. The other retired general, Wiranto, started very slowly, probably because of his unfavourable portrayal in the mass media. Nevertheless, soon after he was nominated as the presidential candidate by Golkar, beating Akbar Tanjung on 20 April 2004, his popularity started rising rapidly in early May 2004.

Unlike the two retired generals, the stars of the three civilian candidates — Megawati, Amien, and Hamzah — were not bright. Megawati's popularity peaked in early April but then dimmed until early June, the beginning of the campaign period. The fortunes of Amien, who was in second position in December 2003, reached bottom in early April 2004. Hamzah also had a better start than Wiranto in December 2003, but since early April, he had always been the least popular candidate.[2]

By 5 July 2004, the polling day, the two generals had been the two most popular candidates, beating the civilians. The rising popularity of Wiranto–Wahid over Megawati–Hasyim had caused some speculation that the run-off election in September would be a battle between two generals. Nevertheless, Megawati–Hasyim seemed to have done much better in the last two weeks before the polling day. Megawati–Hasyim won the second position, and Wiranto–Wahid, the third position. The fact that Megawati had increasingly come out from the palace and approached the public might have contributed to the Megawati–Hasyim victory over Wiranto–Wahid.

However, Wiranto–Wahid refused to accept the election results and brought the case to the constitutional court. They argued that they had lost 5,434,660 votes in twenty-six provinces because of irregularities in counting the votes. If, argued the Wiranto team, the KPU had counted the votes correctly, Wiranto–Wahid's votes would have been 31,721,448, larger than that of Megawati's (31,569,104). Therefore, Wiranto would have become one of the two finalists in the second round. On 10 August 2004, the constitutional court found no irregularities and rejected the petition. Wiranto and his team accepted the verdict. This paved the way for Megawati–Hasyim to face Yudhoyono–Kalla in the second round of the elections.

The Five Pairs

After the results of the April election were announced, preparations for the presidential elections were underway. According to Law No. 23/2003 on Elections of President and Vice President (Article 101), only political parties which obtained five per cent of the total vote and above, or three per cent of the parliamentary seats gained, would be qualified to propose a pair of presidential and vice presidential candidates. Therefore, based on the results from the parliamentary election, only seven political parties (Golkar, PDI-P, PKB, PPP, PD, PKS and PAN) were qualified to nominate their candidates. If small parties obtaining less than five per cent of the votes were interested to nominate their presidential candidates, they were required to join forces with other parties to reach the five per cent requirement. However, on the closing date for nominations (12 May 2004), only six presidential candidates, all of whom were nominated by parties which won more than five per cent of the total votes, were submitted to the General Election Commission (KPU).

The PKS did not submit any names, but close to the polling day of the first round, it threw its support behind PAN's candidates. On 14 May 2004, the KPU confirmed the final list of candidates, which consisted of six pairs: Wiranto–Sollahuddin Wahid, Megawati Soekarnoputri–Hasyim Muzadi, Amien Rais–Siswono Yudho Husodo, Susilo Bambang Yudhoyono–Jusuf Kalla, Hamzah Haz–Agum Gumelar, and Abdurrahman Wahid (commonly known as Gus Dur)–Marwah Daud Ibrahim.

The KPU regulations required all candidates to undergo a medical check-up, including an eye test. On the basis of this medical check-up, on 22 May 2004, the KPU announced that Abdurrahman Wahid failed the test and hence was barred from taking part in the presidential election. Therefore, KPU's Decree No. 36/2004 dated 22 May 2004 approved only five pairs of candidates. The following is some brief but crucial information about the candidates listed in accordance with the sequence from the KPU.

Golkar

The first pair of candidates, Wiranto–Solahuddin Wahid, was nominated by Golkar. As a combination of two Javanese, this pair might have been less attractive to the non-Javanese. Wiranto, born in Yogyakarta on 4 April 1947, was a graduate of the National Military Academy (AMN 1968). He was President Soeharto's aide-de-camp between 1989–93, rapidly rose to the rank of full general and held the position of the Chief of General Staff in the Jakarta Region in 1994–96. He was later appointed Commander of the Army's Strategic Reserve, the Army's Chief of Staff, and Chief of the Army (TNI). During Gus Dur's presidency, he was the minister for defence but was later dismissed due to his alleged abuse of human rights in East Timor. Wiranto was a surprise candidate for Golkar as many expected Akbar Tandjung to represent the party. However, at the Golkar Convention on 20 April 2004, Wiranto defeated Akbar Tanjung.[3] Akbar was greatly disappointed and was accused of refusing to support Wiranto whole-heartedly during the presidential election campaign.

Wiranto's partner, Solahuddin Wahid (better known as Gus Solah), was born in Jombang, East Java on 11 November 1942. He graduated from the Bandung Technological Institute. Receiving personal support from Gus Dur, his older brother and the Nahdlatul Ulama (NU) leader, Wahid was also a deputy of the NU. It is not surprising therefore that the PKB, with NU as the majority of the constituents, officially backed the Wiranto–Wahid pair. In addition, Wahid was deputy chairman of the Indonesian Human Rights Commission and this background might have somewhat helped the reputation of Wiranto.

PDI-P

The second pair of candidates, Megawati Soekarnoputri–Hasyim Muzadi, another combination of two Javanese, was nominated by the PDI-P. This pair might also have been less attractive to the non-Javanese. Megawati, born in Yogyakarta on 23 January 1947, is the eldest daughter of Soekarno, the first president of Indonesia. (See more discussions on Megawati in Chapter 1.) Her running mate was Hasyim Muzadi, born on 8 August 1944 in Tuban (East Java), a cleric who was a leader of the Al-Hikam Islamic Boarding School. He was the general chairman of the NU and became non-active as of 15 May 2004 when he became the vice presidential candidate of Megawati.

At first, the PDS, a party with Christians as its main constituents, wanted to support Yudhoyono–Kalla. However, it changed its mind and supported Megawati–Hasyim because of the Islamic PBB's support for Yudhoyono–Kalla. The combination of Megawati, seen as "secular", and Hasyim, regarded as more "Islamic", might have attracted both secular and Islamic voters. The fact that both are civilians might also have lured those who disliked candidates with a military background.

PAN

The third pair of candidates, Dr Amien Rais–Siswono Yudo Husodo, was also a combination of two Javanese, nominated by PAN. The non-Javanese might also have been less attracted to this pair. They were publicly supported by the PKS, PBR, PNBK, PNIM, PPDI, PSI, and PBSD. Amien was born in Solo, Central Java, on 26 April 1944. (More information on Amien is available in Chapter 1.)

His running mate, Siswono Yudo Husodo, an ethnic Javanese, was born in Mahakam, East Kalimantan on 4 July 1943. During his student days, he was an activist with the GMNI (Gerakan Mahasiswa Nasional Indonesia) and was the Deputy Commander of the Barisan Soekarno — an organization that defended Soekarno. After graduation (1969) he became a businessman, forming a construction company, PT Bangun Cipta Sarana. The chairman of the Indonesian Farmers Association, Siswono was a member of Golkar and served as the minister of state for people's housing (1988–93) and minister for transmigration (1993–98) during the New Order. As Amien had a reputation of being "Islamic" and "reformist" and Siswono of being "nationalist", this pair might have been attractive to the Islamic voters who disliked the New Order and the military.

PD

The fourth pair, Susilo Bambang Yudhoyono–Jusuf Kalla, was nominated by the PD and supported by the PBB and PKPI. Yudhoyono was born on 9 September 1949 in Pacitan, East Java; he graduated from the Indonesian Military Academy in 1973 and received further education in the United States. He retired from the army to be a member of Gus Dur's cabinet, where he first served as minister for energy, and later coordinating minister for political and security affairs. However, he was dismissed by Gus Dur from the cabinet, allegedly refusing to declare martial law. When Megawati succeeded Gus Dur, she invited him to join her cabinet, holding the security affairs position. On 1 March 2004, he withdrew from the cabinet to officially join the race for the presidency.

His running mate, Jusuf Kalla, is a wealthy Muslim businessman of Buginese origins and a member of Golkar. Born in Watampone, Makassar, South Sulawesi, on 15 May 1942, he did his *sarjana* (undergraduate degree) at the Faculty of Economics, Hasanuddin University in 1967. He also obtained a degree from an overseas university. Kalla served as minister for industry and trade in the Abdurrahman Wahid cabinet. He was appointed as the coordinating minister for social welfare in the Megawati cabinet. On April 2004, he withdrew from the cabinet to be nominated as the vice presidential candidate.

This pair was not a combination of two Javanese. The presidential candidate was a Javanese, but the vice presidential candidate was a Buginese, from South Sulawesi; this pair might therefore have been attractive to both the Javanese and non-Javanese. The combination of "secular" Yudhoyono and "Islamic" Kalla might have enhanced the attractiveness of this pair. The military background of Yudhoyono and the civilian background of Kalla might have added another positive dimension.

PPP

The fifth pair, Hamzah Haz–Agum Gumelar, was nominated by the PPP. It was a combination of two non-Javanese and hence it might have attracted more non-Javanese. Hamzah, a non-Javanese, born in the regency of Ketapang, West Kalimantan, on 15 February 1940, was the first Nahdlatul Ulama member to be chairperson of the PPP. Hamzah's record as vice president was not impressive (see Chapter 1 for more discussions on Hamzah).

Agum Gumelar was relatively unknown. He is a Sundanese, born in Tasikmalaya (West Java) on 17 December 1945. He graduated from the National Military Academy (1968), Army Staff College (1985), and Military (ABRI) Staff College (1991). Since 1973, he had served in the military intelligence unit and as head of the special force unit (Kopassus). He was appointed as the minister for transportation in Gus Dur's cabinet, and later took over as the minister for politics and security when Yudhoyono was removed by Gus Dur. Again, when Yudhoyono resigned from Megawati's cabinet, Agum, who was minister for transportation in Megawati's cabinet, filled the vacancy. Later on, he withdrew from Megawati's cabinet to be the vice presidential candidate.

The next two sections assess the support of the parties for the pairs. The discussion utilizes data from the IFES surveys conducted from

December 2003 to the period just after 5 July 2004, which was used to reflect what happened on the polling day of the first round. The official data from the parliamentary and first round of the presidential elections are also utilized to compare the support for the candidates.

The Losing Pairs: Hamzah–Agum, Amien–Siswono, and Wiranto–Wahid

Hamzah–Agum

Hamzah–Agum was in a difficult position with no other parties officially backing their candidacy except Hamzah's own party, the PPP. Worse, they joined the presidential race relatively very late; they officially announced their candidacy only on 12 May 2004, just about two weeks before the campaign period.

As shown in Table 3.2, it was only on polling day (indicated in column "C"), that Hamzah–Agum gained substantial support from their party, the PPP. However, unlike other candidates, the support for Hamzah–Agum was relatively small, given that the PPP was the party which nominated them; they only obtained 29.5 per cent on polling day. The remaining PPP voters were divided among other contenders — 22.7 per cent to Yudhoyono–Kalla, 22.7 per cent to Amien–Siswono, 11.4 per cent to Megawati–Hasyim and 11.4 per cent to Wiranto–Wahid.

Hamzah–Agum were not able to keep the majority of voters from Hamzah's own Islamic party, the PPP. Another big loss for Hamzah–Agum were from the voters of PKB, often seen as an Islamic party, from whom Hamzah–Agum gained 6.8 per cent at the beginning of the campaign but received none on polling day. They did not get any support from the rising Islamic party, the PKS, either. Worse, initially they managed to get around 1.5 per cent from the voters of Golkar and the PDI-P, but lost the support on polling day. They gained very small support from PAN, also often seen as an Islamic party, and some small parties. Due to strong competition from other Islamic candidates and Hamzah's own weak image, he eventually lost the support of many Islamists.

On polling day, Hamzah–Agum only garnered 3.6 million votes, much fewer than the 9.2 million votes the PPP had gained in the parliamentary election. It lost about 1.5 million in West Java and around another 1.5 million in Central Java and East Java together (see Figure 3.1).

TABLE 3.2

Sources of Support for Five Presidential Candidates: Early June – Mid July 2004

Parties	Yudhoyono			Megawati			Wiranto			Amien			Hamzah			Did Not Vote		
	A	B	C	A	B	C	A	B	C	A	B	C	A	B	C	A	B	C
GOLKAR	45.2	39.1	40.2	6.5	5.1	3.0	28.6	38.4	48.4	4.0	5.1	4.2	1.6	1.1	0.0	14.1	11.2	4.2
PDI-P	21.1	22.3	23.7	54.2	59.2	71.1	4.2	3.8	0.8	3.5	1.2	0.8	1.4	0.0	0.0	15.6	13.5	3.6
PPP	48.8	39.4	22.7	2.3	3.0	11.4	9.3	7.1	11.4	2.3	10.1	22.7	16.3	26.3	29.5	21.0	14.1	2.3
PKB	47.7	47.4	37.5	2.3	5.9	19.2	15.9	18.4	30.8	3.4	2.6	3.8	6.8	2.6	0.0	23.9	23.1	8.7
PD	89.2	87.3	89.5	0.0	2.4	0.7	3.2	3.2	0.7	1.1	2.0	0.7	0.0	0.0	0.0	6.5	5.1	8.4
PKS	39.6	40.2	29.0	6.3	1.0	9.7	8.3	7.2	21.0	29.2	39.2	35.5	0.0	2.1	0.0	16.6	10.3	4.8
PAN	14.3	14.7	9.8	0.0	0.9	1.1	4.4	2.6	4.3	78.0	71.6	81.5	0.0	0.9	1.1	3.3	9.3	2.2
PBB	28.6	48.6	40.0	42.9	2.7	6.7	28.6	10.8	6.7	0.0	18.9	33.3	0.0	5.4	0.0	0.0	13.6	13.3
PBR	37.5	52.2	54.5	0.0	4.3	0.0	25.0	17.4	36.4	25.0	26.1	0.0	0.0	0.0	0.0	12.5	0.0	9.1
PDS	55.6	33.3	41.7	16.7	33.3	58.3	11.1	22.2	0.0	5.6	0.0	0.0	0.0	0.0	0.0	11.0	11.2	0.0
Others	53.2	59.1	51.1	13.3	6.0	21.3	11.4	10.4	4.2	3.8	9.6	12.8	3.8	1.7	2.1	14.5	13.2	8.5
Secret	39.2	36.1	13.2	8.6	6.4	0.9	6.1	7.1	15.8	2.4	4.9	2.6	0.4	1.9	0.0	43.3	43.6	67.5
No Response	23.5	23.8	30.0	0.0	2.4	6.7	0.0	2.4	16.7	5.9	4.8	3.3	5.9	2.4	0.0	64.7	64.2	44.3
Abstain	–	–	14.1	–	–	4.7	–	–	1.6	–	–	12.5	–	–	0.0	–	–	67.1

Note: A refers to 4–9 June 2004; B to 17–26 June 2004; and C to 7–14 July 2004.
   "C" may be used as proxy to what happened on polling day.
Source: Compiled from IFES (2004f) and IFES (2004g).

FIGURE 3.1
Number of Votes for Hamzah and PPP by Province:
April and July 2004

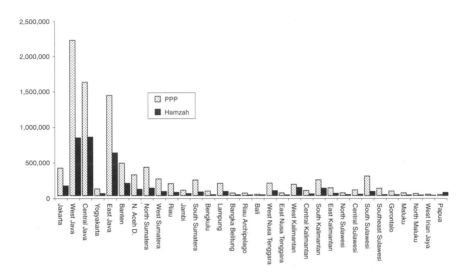

Source: Table 3.3 and Appendix 3.1.

Amien–Siswono

In the April election, PAN, Amien's party, gained 7.3 million votes. Party leaders of the following six small parties: the Partai Bintang Reformasi (PBR or Reformed Star Party), Partai National Banteng Kemerdekaan (PNBK or Freedom Bull Nationalist Party), PNI Marhaenisme (PNIM or Marhaenism Indonesian National Party), Partai Buruh Sosial Demokrat (PBSD or Social Democratic Labour Party), Partai Penegak Demokrasi Indonesia (PPDI or Indonesian Democratic Vanguard Party) and Partai Sarikat Indonesia (PSI or Indonesian Unity Party), declared on 28 May 2004 that their parties would support the Amien–Siswono pair for the July presidential election. Later, the PKS leader also declared its support of this pair. Each of these parties only obtained, respectively, 2.8 million, 1.2 million, 0.9 million, 0.6 million, 0.9 million, 0.7 million, 3.1 million and 8.3 million votes in April.

During the campaign, Amien–Siswono received large support from PAN, which nominated them. They garnered around 75 per cent of the PAN votes. However, about 25 per cent did not favour Amien–Siswono, implying that the pair had not been so successful in consolidating the full support from the PAN voters. On the other hand, the PAN voters were also unlikely to vote for both the then president (Megawati) and vice president (Hamzah) — indeed PAN's voters for Megawati–Hasyim and Hamzah–Agum amounted to only about 1.1 per cent.

Next, Amien–Siswono attracted only about 30 to 40 per cent of the PKS voters. The relatively low support from the PKS voters had been as predicted, because there were two opposing camps within the PKS from the beginning, one supporting Wiranto–Wahid and the other Amien–Siswono, both with equally strong arguments (Piliang 2004). The PKS had officially announced its backing of Amien–Siswono relatively late on 30 June 2004, just a few days before polling day.

This late support might have cost Amien–Siswono a significant loss of potential votes. Indeed, as shown in Table 3.2, during the last two weeks before the polling day (compare columns B and C), the support from the PKS voters for Wiranto–Wahid had increased, probably at the expense of those for Amien–Siswono and more importantly, for Yudhoyono–Kalla. In addition, in the last two weeks, the support from the PKS voters for Megawati had also risen from a very low 1.0 per cent to 9.7 per cent, probably reflecting PAN voters who did not like a president with a military background. Yet, the support of the PKS voters for Amien–Siswono could have been worse if there had been no official support from the PKS. Despite this, the largest support from the PKS on polling day was still for Amien–Siswono (35.5 per cent), compared to Wiranto–Wahid (21 per cent) and Yudhoyono–Kalla (29 per cent).

Amien–Siswono also received growing support from the PBB, PPP and "other parties". Interestingly, on polling day, they did not get any support from the voters of the PBR, which had officially backed the pair, though they earned 25.0 per cent of the PBR votes during the campaign period. Wiranto–Wahid might have captured the PBR voters in the last two weeks of the campaign period, probably showing PBR's "pragmatism" in voting for those who were more likely to win, as Wiranto–Wahid's popularity had exceeded that of Amien–Siswono during the campaign period.

In the early campaign period, Amien–Siswono obtained support from 5.6 per cent of the voters for the PDS, a party with Christians as the main constituents — but the one-month campaign had completely eroded this support. On the other hand, though the PBB officially supported Yudhoyono–Kalla, 33.3 per cent of the voters of the PBB supported Amien–Siswono, indicating that the voters did not necessarily follow party lines.

Had all members of the parties backing Amien–Siswono followed their political elites' commitment, Amien–Siswono would have gained at least 22.7 million votes. However, as discussed above, many of the voters for the parties backing Amien–Siswono did not vote for this pair, who secured only 17.4 million votes. They lost 5.3 million votes, about 25 per cent of the votes they should have obtained. Figure 3.2 shows that they only managed to gain more votes than expected in Nanggroe Aceh Darussalam and West Sumatra. In the provinces where the parties had more voters, this pair failed to attract them.

Wiranto–Wahid

Wiranto–Wahid's star kept rising until the first round of the presidential elections. Their popularity surpassed that of Megawati–Hasyim in the early campaign month and the gap between the two became larger in late June, just about ten days before the election.

Table 3.2 shows that during the campaign period and on polling day, Wiranto–Wahid consistently gained increasing support from the voters who voted for Golkar and the PKB. These two parties had

FIGURE 3.2
**Number of Votes for Amien–Siswono and the
Supporting Parties by Province:
April and July 2004**

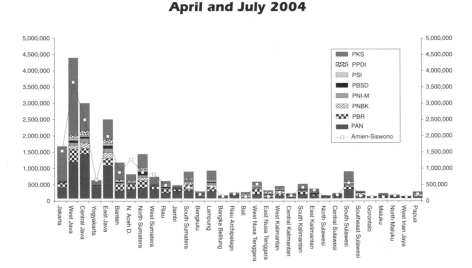

Source: Table 3.3 and Appendix 3.1.

publicly and officially endorsed the candidacies of Wiranto–Wahid. They secured the highest support from Golkar, almost 50 per cent on polling day. Nevertheless, this achievement can be seen as a small success given that Golkar had officially nominated this pair. Wiranto had not been able to consolidate Golkar's vote, and it had been rumoured that Akbar, the chairperson of Golkar, did not support Wiranto's nomination wholeheartedly. On the other hand, Yudhono–Kalla had secured 40.2 per cent of the Golkar voters, partly because of Kalla's influence on Golkar.

During the last two weeks before election day, Wiranto–Wahid and Megawati–Hasyim had enjoyed rising support from the PKB voters, while Yudhoyono–Kalla and Hamzah–Agum had diminishing support from the PKB. Nevertheless, despite the rising support from the PKB for Wiranto–Wahid and Megawati–Hasyim, Yudhoyono–Kalla still maintained the highest support from the PKB voters, even more than that for Wiranto–Wahid, who were officially backed by the PKB, indicating that PKB voters did not necessarily follow the party line.

The strong support from Gus Dur and some respected *kyais* (scholars of Islam) to vote for Wiranto–Wahid had not been successful in bringing most of the PKB voters to choose this pair. As seen in Table 3.3, in East Java, the PKB's stronghold province, Wiranto–Wahid only gained just a little more than half of the expected votes (9 million). The voters threw their support behind Yudhoyono, probably due to the fact that he himself was born in Pacitan, East Java and his mother resides in Blitar, another city in the province.

Nevertheless, the Wahid candidacy, Gus Dur's and some other *kyais'* support had, to some extent, attracted PKB voters. Wiranto–Wahid had then successfully consolidated this strength in some key regions, especially in Java. This success, as argued by the IFES (2004*g*), was one of the possible explanations of the rising support for Wiranto–Wahid in the last two weeks of the campaign month. Wiranto–Wahid seemed to have been able to take some of the Yudhoyono–Kalla's popularity away, especially in the provinces with traditionally strong PKB supporters.

For example, in Central Java, Wiranto–Wahid garnered only 10 per cent in the pre-election survey, and yet they secured 21 per cent during the election. These increases took place at the expense of Yudhoyono–Kalla, who secured 46 per cent of the votes before the election, but only 29 per cent during the election. In East Java, Wiranto–Wahid garnered merely 19 per cent during the pre-election survey, but they managed to reach 24 per cent on election day. On the other hand,

TABLE 3.3
Number of Votes in the First Round

No.	Province	1 Wiranto–Wahid	2 Megawati–Hasyim	3 Amien–Siswono	4 Yudhoyono–Kalla	5 Hamzah–Agum	Valid Votes
1	N. Aceh Darussalam	204,534	120,226	1,195,823	519,197	88,836	2,128,616
2	North Sumatera	934,213	2,233,777	798,790	1,523,612	105,687	5,596,079
3	West Sumatera	610,847	121,254	741,811	518,648	57,228	2,049,788
4	Riau	504,017	460,328	397,761	677,761	44,092	2,083,959
5	Jambi	364,651	273,925	155,974	520,145	28,437	1,343,132
6	South Sumatera	640,294	1,127,608	341,716	1,241,095	50,644	3,401,357
7	Bengkulu	253,986	155,657	121,483	196,057	12,480	739,663
8	Lampung	881,715	896,581	359,285	1,430,729	58,297	3,626,607
9	Bangka Belitung	82,250	179,777	58,759	165,657	11,656	498,099
10	Riau Archipelago	81,816	153,138	128,551	224,334	9,437	597,276
11	Jakarta	543,450	1,235,272	1,452,327	2,083,950	136,190	5,451,189
12	West Java	5,341,526	5,095,705	3,562,173	7,100,175	810,519	21,910,098
13	Central Java	3,943,032	5,807,127	2,409,138	5,276,432	820,273	18,256,002
14	Yogyakarta	334,067	557,133	558,068	576,012	28,293	2,053,573
15	East Java	5,076,454	5,896,278	1,902,254	7,458,399	599,806	20,933,191
16	Banten	922,299	1,193,414	796,758	1,706,548	172,971	4,791,990
17	Bali	210,784	1,115,788	48,472	654,127	9,791	2,038,962
18	West Nusa Tenggara	723,484	223,204	436,073	715,838	68,382	2,166,981

19	East Nusa Tenggara	432,823	1,344,116	58,341	312,777	8,757	2,156,814
20	West Kalimantan	415,492	821,577	185,097	477,724	113,244	2,013,134
21	Central Kalimantan	170,193	296,335	88,439	303,123	23,976	882,066
22	South Kalimantan	353,732	211,881	339,993	600,156	103,429	1,609,191
23	East Kalimantan	246,715	337,458	255,665	558,900	31,459	1,430,197
24	North Sulawesi	451,663	389,135	47,309	355,436	13,380	1,256,923
25	Central Sulawesi	455,167	119,917	101,877	539,624	17,865	1,234,450
26	South Sulawesi	678,445	381,385	476,483	2,854,774	57,728	4,448,815
27	Southeast Sulawesi	361,386	108,905	74,496	398,544	11,907	955,238
28	Gorontalo	402,162	39,647	39,569	31,210	12,624	525,212
29	Maluku	288,091	269,611	40,392	100,748	8,887	707,729
30	North Maluku	181,373	98,459	75,404	102,353	6,272	463,861
31	West Irian Jaya	38,425	102,191	18,221	148,675	3,538	311,050
32	Papua	157,702	202,295	126,429	465,424	43,776	995,626
	National	26,286,788	31,569,104	17,392,931	39,838,184	3,569,861	118,656,868

continued on next page

TABLE 3.3 – cont'd
Votes in Percentages

No.	Province	1 Wiranto–Wahid	2 Megawati–Hasyim	3 Amien–Siswono	4 Yudhoyono–Kalla	5 Hamzah–Agum	Valid Votes
1	N. Aceh Darussalam	9.61	5.65	56.18	24.39	4.17	100
2	North Sumatera	16.69	39.92	14.27	27.23	1.89	100
3	West Sumatera	29.80	5.92	36.19	25.30	2.79	100
4	Riau	24.19	22.09	19.09	32.52	2.12	100
5	Jambi	27.15	20.39	11.61	38.73	2.12	100
6	South Sumatera	18.82	33.15	10.05	36.49	1.49	100
7	Bengkulu	34.34	21.04	16.42	26.51	1.69	100
8	Lampung	24.31	24.72	9.91	39.45	1.61	100
9	Bangka Belitung	16.51	36.09	11.80	33.26	2.34	100
10	Riau Archipelago	13.70	25.64	21.52	37.56	1.58	100
11	Jakarta	9.97	22.66	26.64	38.23	2.50	100
12	West Java	24.38	23.26	16.26	32.41	3.70	100
13	Central Java	21.60	31.81	13.20	28.90	4.49	100
14	Yogyakarta	16.27	27.13	27.18	28.05	1.38	100
15	East Java	24.25	28.17	9.09	35.63	2.87	100
16	Banten	19.25	24.90	16.63	35.61	3.61	100
17	Bali	10.34	54.72	2.38	32.08	0.48	100
18	West Nusa Tenggara	33.39	10.30	20.12	33.03	3.16	100
19	East Nusa Tenggara	20.07	62.32	2.70	14.50	0.41	100
20	West Kalimantan	20.64	40.81	9.19	23.73	5.63	100

22	Central Kalimantan	19.29	33.60	10.03	34.37	2.72	100
21	South Kalimantan	21.98	13.17	21.13	37.30	6.43	100
23	East Kalimantan	17.25	23.60	17.88	39.08	2.20	100
24	North Sulawesi	35.93	30.96	3.76	28.28	1.06	100
25	Central Sulawesi	36.87	9.71	8.25	43.71	1.45	100
26	South Sulawesi	15.25	8.57	10.71	64.17	1.30	100
27	Southeast Sulawesi	37.83	11.40	7.80	41.72	1.25	100
28	Gorontalo	76.57	7.55	7.53	5.94	2.40	100
29	Maluku	40.71	38.10	5.71	14.24	1.26	100
30	North Maluku	39.10	21.23	16.26	22.07	1.35	100
32	West Irian Jaya	12.35	32.85	5.86	47.80	1.14	100
31	Papua	15.84	20.32	12.70	46.75	4.40	100
	National	22.15	26.61	14.66	33.57	3.01	100

Source: Compiled and calculated from <www.kpu.go.id>.

Yudhoyono–Kalla gained 48 per cent in the pre-election survey, but only secured 36 per cent on election day. Similar results can also be seen in West Java, where Wiranto–Wahid garnered 15 per cent in the pre-election survey and 21 per cent on polling day. As in East Java, Yudhoyono–Kalla earned the most but their popularity decreased from 45 per cent in the pre-election survey to 34 per cent in the election in this province.

Nevertheless, Wiranto–Wahid received fewer votes than expected from the political arithmetic, as indicated by the number of voters from Golkar and PKB, which supported the pair. If the voters had fully followed the party lines, Wiranto–Wahid would have gained at least 36.4 million votes in the July presidential election. It turned out that they only garnered 26.3 million votes. Therefore, Wiranto–Wahid lost 10.1 million votes, almost 30 per cent of what had been expected. This may indicate that the party machinery did not provide sufficient support for their candidates.

As can be seen from Figure 3.3, a clear example was in South Sulawesi, the Golkar stronghold, where the votes did not go to

FIGURE 3.3

Number of Votes for Wiranto–Wahid and the Supporting Parties by Province: April and July 2004

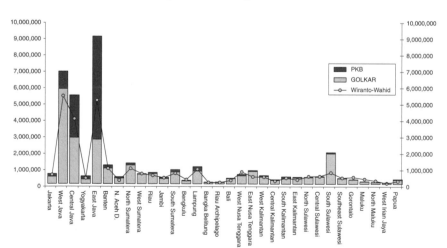

Source: Table 3.3 and Appendix 3.1.

Wiranto–Wahid. In South Sulawesi, this pair should have gained nearly two million votes, but they only managed to secure less than one million. Instead, their expected votes might have mostly gone to another retired general, Yudhoyono, and his running mate, Kalla. The fact that Kalla was born in South Sulawesi might have been a very strong factor in this province. Wiranto–Wahid earned more votes than expected only in Bengkulu, West Nusa Tenggara, Gorontalo, Maluku, and North Maluku.

The Winning Pairs:
Megawati–Hasyim and Yudhoyono–Kalla

Megawati–Hasyim

Table 3.1 shows that Megawati–Hasyim's popularity started picking up in the later part of the campaign period (June 2004) and rose rapidly towards polling day. As shown in Table 3.2, Megawati–Hasyim received greater and increasing support from the voters of the PDI-P and PDS — the two parties that officially backed them. This pair received more than 70 per cent from the PDI-P's voters and almost 60 per cent from the PDS voters in the first round of the presidential elections. The PDS voters initially gave their support to three candidates: Yudhoyono–Kalla, Megawati–Hasyim, and Amien–Siswono before the election. During the election, they voted either for Yudhoyono–Kalla or Megawati–Hasyim only, with more votes for Megawati–Hasyim.

The percentage of support for Megawati–Hasyim from Islamic parties such as the PPP, PKB, PKS, and other parties had also more than doubled during the last ten days. Nevertheless, and not surprisingly, the PPP support for Megawati–Hasyim was not higher than their support for their own pair of candidates, Hamzah–Agum. The PKB support of one-fifth for Megawati–Hasyim was larger than that from the PPP on election day.

As argued by the IFES (2004g), one likely explanation for the increase in votes for Megawati–Hasyim was their ability to enhance support in some key regions, particularly in Java, in the last two weeks before the campaign period ended. Their campaign had been able to attract voters of the more "secular" PDI-P and "Christian" PDS, which officially backed them; they also gained rising support from some "Islamic" parties. In other words, Megawati–Hasyim's voters might have been relatively more pluralistic.

Megawati–Hasyim obtained only 11 per cent in the pre-election survey in Central Java, but this rose to a much larger percentage (31 per cent) on election day. In East Java, Megawati–Hasyim earned only 13 per cent in the pre-election survey, yet gained 28 per cent during the election. In West Java, Megawati–Hasyim secured 16 per cent in the pre-election survey and 23 per cent on polling day. IFES also reported that in Bali, East Nusa Tenggara, and West Nusa Tenggara, Megawati–Hasyim earned about 29 per cent in each region, a similar percentage gained by Yudhoyono–Kalla. Yet, during the election, Megawati–Hasyim garnered 55 per cent of the votes in these regions, much larger than the 34 per cent secured by Yudhoyono–Kalla.

However, they continuously lost the support from those who voted for Golkar, whose candidates were Wiranto–Wahid. At first, the support for them from Golkar's voters was small at only 6.5 per cent. Megawati–Hasyim's support from the PBB in early June was high, at more than 40 per cent. As this party threw its support behind Yudhoyono–Kalla, the support suddenly declined to a very low 2.7 per cent, during the campaign period, but on polling day it increased, and Megawati–Hasyim were supported by 6.7 per cent of the PBB's voters.

The support for Megawati–Hasyim from the PD voters was slim. Initially, Megawati–Hasyim had not gained any support from them. However, by the end of the campaign period, they obtained 2.4 per cent of the PD vote. Yet, it then dropped to 0.7 per cent on election day, confirming speculation that the PD voters were mostly those who were not happy with the PDI-P and Megawati.

Nevertheless, Megawati–Hasyim were increasingly popular among the independent voters. They obtained 31.6 million votes, 8.2 million more than expected (21 million from the PDI-P and 2.4 million from the PDS) in the July election. In other words, Megawati–Hasyim had been able to receive support from outside the PDI-P and PDS. The pair also regained the PDI-P 1999 victory in North Sumatra, and grabbed victory from Golkar in East Nusa Tenggara, Maluku and West Kalimantan. In Bangka-Belitung, the pair even beat the Islamist Crescent Star Party (PBB), Yusril Ihza Mahendra's party, which openly declared backing Yudhoyono in the July and September elections (see Figure 3.4).

Yudhoyono–Kalla

Yudhoyono–Kalla's popularity reached its peak at 45.0 per cent in early June but started to drop slightly to 43.5 per cent in late June, just about

FIGURE 3.4
Number of Votes for Megawati–Hasyim and the
Supporting Parties by Province:
April and July 2004

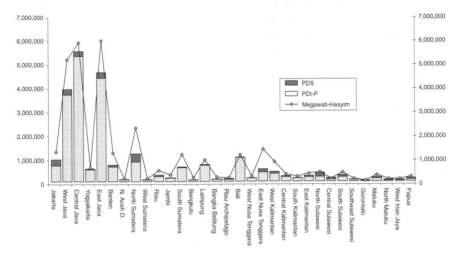

Source: Table 3.3 and Appendix 3.1.

ten days before the elections. Yudhoyono–Kalla suffered a further, larger, drop in the first presidential elections, gaining only 33.6 per cent of the votes. The campaign period seemed to have benefited other pairs, particularly Megawati–Hasyim, more than Yudhoyono–Kalla.

Yudhoyono–Kalla received consistently very high support (almost 90 per cent) from the PD, the party which nominated them, during the campaign period and the election day, indicating strong loyalty from the PD's voters. Their support from the PBR, a small Islamic party which officially backed Amien–Siswono, increased during the campaign period, from 37.5 per cent in the early part of the campaign period to 52.2 per cent by the end of the campaign period and to 54.5 per cent on polling day. Though not by much, the support from the PDI-P voters for Yudhoyono–Kalla also increased during the campaign period, from 21.2 per cent in the early part to 22.3 per cent in the late part, and 23.7 per cent on polling day — perhaps revealing Yudhoyono–Kalla's ability to sway some PDI-P's voters away from Megawati–Hasyim. On the other hand, support from the PPP and PKB voters had declined from the early part of the campaign to the polling day; from 48.8 to 22.7 per cent among PPP's voters and from 47.7 to 37.5 per cent among PKB's voters.

Support from voters from other parties fluctuated. Though the PBB officially supported the nomination of Yudhoyono–Kalla, only less than half voted for this pair. PBB votes actually rose during the campaign period (from 28.6 to 48.6 per cent), but then declined to 40.0 per cent on election day, indicating the PBB voters did not necessarily follow the official backing of the PBB leaders. The rumoured internal conflict within the PBB might have caused this pair to retain only less than half of the PBB voters.

The swinging of preferences for presidential and vice presidential candidates, and perhaps the confusion of the voters, can also be shown in the support for Yudhoyono–Kalla from the voters of the PKS and PAN — which first rose (though by not much) and then declined, from 39.6 to 29.0 per cent among PKS' voters, and from 14.3 to 9.8 per cent among PAN's voters. A slightly different pattern could be identified among Golkar's and the PDS' voters — the support first declined and then rose but was still lower than the initial support. Yudhoyono–Kalla initially received 45.2 per cent of Golkar's voters and ended up obtaining 40.2 per cent from them on election day; their support from PDS' voters started at 55.6 per cent but dropped to 41.7 per cent on election day. It should be mentioned here that the PDS publicly supported Megawati–Hasyim.

The IFES argued that the decline in the support for Yudhoyono–Kalla and the rise in the support for other candidates (especially Megawati–Hasyim and Wiranto–Wahid) in the last two weeks before the election were also due to the shift of party supporters to their own presidential candidates. It found that 38.4 per cent of Golkar voters chose Wiranto–Wahid in the pre-election, and rose to 48.4 per cent on election day. Among the PKB, which also supported Wiranto–Wahid, 18.4 per cent supported Wiranto–Wahid prior to the election and rose to 30.8 per cent on election day. At the same time the support for Yudhoyono–Kalla from the PKB declined from 47.4 per cent in the pre-election survey to 37.5 per cent on election day.

The support from the PPP for Yudhoyono–Kalla also dropped, from 39.4 to 22.7 per cent, and perhaps the bulk of the drop went to Amien–Siswono. On the other hand, the support from Golkar was almost the same, from 39.1 to 40.2 per cent; the PDI-P, from 22.3 per cent to 23.7 per cent; the PD, from 87.3 to 89.5 per cent; and the PKS, from 40.2 to 29.0 per cent. Yudhoyono–Kalla also suffered a loss of votes from smaller parties: the PBB, which had openly given their support to

Yudhoyono–Kalla, dropped from 49 to 40 per cent; and from other smaller parties, from 59 to 51 per cent.

In short, in the last two weeks before the first round of the elections, Yudhoyono–Kalla had lost some support from "Islamic" parties (the PPP, PKB, PKS, and PAN) and other parties. Yudhoyono–Kalla also lost support from the PBB, another Islamic party, which had publicly supported them before the July election. On the other hand, Yudhoyono–Kalla received increasing support, though relatively little, from the "secular" Golkar, PDI-P, and PD, and the "Christian" PDS. Because the rise in support was much smaller than the decline, in total Yudhoyono–Kalla suffered a significant loss in support during the last two weeks before the polling date, though they still maintained the first winner position.

The election results of Yudhoyono–Kalla show that the "political arithmetic" was wrong because of the voters' growing independence in choosing a party and a presidential-vice presidential pair. If Yudhoyono–Kalla had simply depended on the parliamentary voters of the PD, PBB, and PKPI, which supported this pair, they would have gained only about 12.9 million votes. However, the manual tally showed that Yudhoyono and his running mate were the front-runners securing 39.8 million votes — 26.9 million more than expected. They won in eighteen out of thirty-two provinces, mostly where Golkar gained in April. They gained much more than is shown in the "political arithmetic", especially in the island of Java and the province of South Sulawesi (see Figure 3.5).

Why Yudhoyono?

Though both Megawati–Hasyim and Yudhoyono–Kalla gained from the increasing independence of the voters, it was Yudhoyono–Kalla who reaped most of the benefit, given that Yudhoyono's party only garnered 7.5 per cent in the parliamentary election. This meteoric popularity of Yudhoyono can be examined using the results from a focus group discussion conducted by the National Democratic Institute for International Affairs during May 2004, before the first round of the elections, in seven provinces: Jakarta, West Java, Central Java, Papua, West Irian Jaya, North Sulawesi, and East Kalimantan (for more details of the results, see NDI 2004).

The study shows that the participants were generally unhappy with conditions in Indonesia, especially in relation to economic matters such

FIGURE 3.5
Number of Votes for Yudhoyono–Kalla and the
Supporting Parties by Province:
April and July 2004

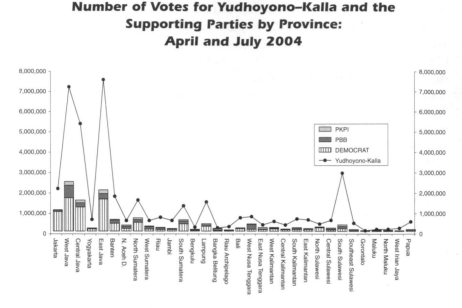

Source: Table 3.3 and Appendix 3.1.

as rising prices and difficulty in finding desired jobs. It is therefore not difficult to understand that this unhappiness had been easily translated into unhappiness towards Megawati. NDI (2004) explained that Megawati had a "unique burden". Among all presidential and vice presidential candidates, she was the only one held responsible for all undesirable things under her administration, though some of the other candidates held important positions in the Megawati administration.[4] This dissatisfaction towards Megawati caused some voters to vote "anyone else but Megawati" (*asal bukan Mega*).

It should be mentioned, however, that though the participants of the study were not happy, they were by no means unaware of Megawati's achievements. They had enjoyed improvements around them — they were proud of many road constructions, new shopping malls, and infrastructure. They were satisfied with the political transition to greater civil liberties, including the policy and implementation of regional autonomy.

Indeed, Megawati had done her job in the economic field during her three-year administration. The economy grew at 3.5 per cent in

2001, and it had grown faster at 3.7 per cent in 2002, and 4.5 per cent in 2003. The inflation rate had been down from 12.6 per cent in 2001 to 10.0 per cent in 2002, and 5.1 per cent in 2003. The rupiah has been strengthening from about Rp. 10,450 to one US dollar in December 2001 to about Rp. 8,500 in December 2003, and the interest rate, measured with a one-month central bank rate, had declined from 17.6 per cent in December 2001 to 13.0 per cent in December 2002 and 8.3 per cent in December 2003. Similarly, the political situation was relatively stable.

However, the problem was that perhaps people had expected too much from Megawati, and the fact that the Megawati camp had failed to communicate her achievements in both the economic and political fields during her administration. During the campaign, Megawati had left her "cocoon", and she transformed herself into a "different" Megawati, a new Megawati who had been much closer to the people than during most of the time when she had been the president. This transformation of Megawati might have been credited for her rising popularity, but it was too little and too late.[5]

Participants from the focus group study gave more weight to personal qualities than policy statements or party affiliation when they decided whom they would vote for president. They complained about many "small" but annoying corruptions they experienced in their routine daily life, from getting jobs, bribes for routine official administrative transactions and services. Yudhoyono was believed to be able to clean up all these things.

The participants wanted an honest president, because they believed that it was the only way to eradicate the widespread corruption in Indonesia. They wanted honesty and values, not necessarily religious. Yudhoyono was seen as a man who was neither overly religious nor anti-Muslim. Some participants were also not very comfortable with a woman as president, though not necessarily because of religious reasons.

Yudhoyono had been the rising star among the participants. He was seen as a person of integrity, sufficient competency and "authoritative bearing". His military background was seen more as an asset than a liability. The word most cited in favour of Yudhoyono is that he was very *tegas*, meaning "firm" and able to take decisive action: he was expected to be *tegas* to overcome the KKN (corruption, collusion, and nepotism) — the most consistently mentioned problem Indonesia has to solve. There were no negative sides to Yudhoyono in the eyes of the participants who took part in the focus group study.

Among the participants, when choosing one of the five candidates for the first round of the elections, they preferred Yudhoyono either in the first place or second place. In short, he had broad appeal in the study. This is in contrast to Wiranto and Megawati, whom some participants never wanted to consider as their president.

Concluding Remarks

On 5 July 2004, Indonesians experienced their first direct presidential election. On Monday, 26 July 2004, with Decree No. 79/2004 the KPU officially endorsed two pairs of candidates — Megawati–Hasyim and Yudhoyono–Kalla — to vie for the presidency in the 20 September run-off. None could get the 50 per cent magic mark in the first round to avoid the run-off and the top two moved on to the second round. As shown in Figure 3.6 Yudhoyono–Kalla won their victory in more than half of the provinces, while Megawati–Hasyim won in six provinces only, namely, North Sumatra, Bangka-Belitung, Central Java, Bali, East Nusa Tenggara, and West Kalimantan. Wiranto–Wahid also won in six provinces, Bengkulu, West Nusa Tenggara, North Sulawesi, Gorontalo,

FIGURE 3.6
The Winning Candidates in the First Round

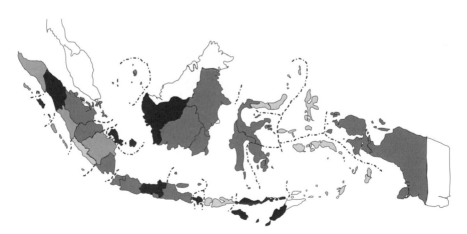

■ Yudhoyono-Kalla   ■ Megawati-Hasyim   □ Wiranto-Wahid   ■ Amien-Siswono

Source: Drawn from Table 3.3.

Maluku and North Maluku; and Amien–Siswono won only in two provinces, Aceh and West Sumatra. Hamzah–Agum failed to win in any province.

As mentioned in Chapter 1, a conservative estimate has been made that there were about 150 million eligible voters in the 2004 elections.[6] In the July election, 2.7 million were invalid votes and about 28.7 million were Golput. The number of Golput in the July election was larger than that in the April election, indicating an increasing number of eligible voters who felt their votes did not make any important contribution to the country. Again, as in the April election, the number of Golput could be higher if some of the invalid votes were from those who did it purposely. Unlike in the April election where Golput was the first winner, Golput occupied third position in the July election, after Yudhoyono–Kalla and Megawati–Hasyim.

As discussed in this chapter, the voters' choice of the presidential-vice presidential candidates did not necessarily follow their choice of the parties which supported the candidates. This was the first time that Indonesians could choose their own president directly, and that they did not have to follow the interest of their political leaders. Golkar was the winner in the April election, but Wiranto–Wahid could not even go to the final round in the September election. Though the PD was in fifth position in April, Yudhoyono–Kalla won the first place in July. PAN was the seventh in April, but Amien–Siswono managed to be the fourth winner in July. The PDI-P with Megawati–Hasyim was the only exception — their performances in April and July were consistent. The PDI-P was in second place in April; Megawati–Hasyim, also came in second in July.

Wiranto–Wahid, Amien–Siswono, and Hamzah–Agum should have obtained more votes in July, had the party supporters followed the results of the parliamentary elections. Megawati–Hasyim, and particularly Yudhoyono–Kalla, had gained much more than what they should have if the voters had given their support in line with the decision of the political leaders.

The Yudhoyono–Kalla pair benefited greatly from the independence of the voters; Yudhoyono's personality also won many admirers, much more than his vision did. Not surprisingly, this presidential election was more a contest of individual popularity, rather than the party or even the programme and vision of the candidates. Each candidate spent a lot of money in order to remain visible in the public eye, and the mass media might have played an important role in shaping the positive image of Yudhoyono.

The first two elections in 2004 showed that the commitment made among the political élites had not necessarily been translated into the decisions made by the individual voters. Wiranto–Solahuddin, Amien–Siswono, and Hamzah–Agum had gained less than what the supporting parties had obtained in the parliamentary election. On the other hand, Megawati–Hasyim and particularly Yudhoyono–Kalla had benefited much from the rising "independence" of the voters.

Voters behaved differently when choosing a political party in the April election and when choosing a pair of presidential and vice presidential candidates in the July election. They became more independent, and did not necessarily follow the party lines. This was the first time in Indonesian politics that individual voters had much greater power in deciding the president and vice president — in constrast to the Soekarno and Soeharto eras when individual voters played no role.

Notes

1. Derwin Pereira, "Who will be Mega's Running Mate?", *Straits Times*, 7 November 2003.
2 . Not surprisingly, he was not happy with results from polling surveys, showing his low popularity. (*Tempo* 2004).
3. Initially, there were six presidential candidates from Golkar: The party leader Akbar Tandjung, businessman Aburizal Bakrie, Coordinating Minister for the People's Welfare Jusuf Kalla, former Army's Special Forces Commander Prabowo Subianto, media tycoon Surya Paloh and former Indonesian military commander General (ret) Wiranto (*Pikiran Rakyat* 2004). Later, Kalla withdrew his candidacy and joined Yudhoyono to be the vice presidential candidate. On 20 April 2004, Golkar held its convention to nominate the presidential candidate. During the election process, at first it was strongly believed that Golkar General Chairman Akbar Tanjung was highly likely to emerge victorious. But in the second round of convention voting, Wiranto won 315 votes, surpassing Akbar, who managed only 227 (*Kompas* 2004b). None of the presidential candidates won a majority of 50 per cent of votes plus one vote in the first round. Wiranto had been in second place (137 votes), after Akbar, who had 147. Aburizal Bakrie won 118 votes, followed by Surya Paloh with 77 votes and Lt. Gen. (ret) Prabowo Subianto with 39 votes. Twenty-eight votes were invalid and one vote was an abstention (*Kompas* 2004a).
4. Yudhoyono was the coordinating minister for politics and security until March 2004. Kalla served as the coordinating minister for people's welfare. Hamzah was the vice president, Agum the minister of transportation, and

Amien the chairperson of the People's Consultative Assembly which monitors and approves the policies and implementation of the government.

5. The failure of Megawati's camp in communicating with the grassroots can be illustrated with a conversation with a *wong cilik* (common people) in Batam in the province of Riau Archipelago, just after the parliamentary elections.[5] She was financially much better off than during the Soeharto era, but she still complained about the rising prices. When it was explained to her that her rising nominal income was partly because of the rising prices, she still could not understand and she kept saying, "If the prices were still as low as before, as promised by Megawati, I would have been much better off financially." Well, a lecture on introductory macroeconomics is far beyond her grasp!

6. IndonesianFamous.com "Susilo–Kalla dan Megawati–Hasyim Maju ke Putaran 2 Pemilu Presiden" mentioned that 121.3 million eligible voters had exercised their right to vote.

4

A New President Emerges
The Second Round

With only two presidential candidates left for the final round of elections in September, the competition had become tougher. This chapter examines voters' decisions on whether to choose the presidential candidate who had a "proven track record" (Megawati–Hasyim) or the one who promised change (Yudhoyono–Kalla). It compares their performances in the first and second rounds of the presidential elections and discusses their popularity. It is followed by an assessment of the political coalitions' performance, as well as the background characteristics and the expectation of their voters.

The Choice between "Proven Track Record" and "Change"

The second round of the presidential elections was not a competition of two retired generals, but between a retired general and a civilian, and between "the proven track record" (*sudah teruji*), the key words from Megawati–Hasyim's camp, and "change" (*perubahan*), the slogan of Yudhoyono–Kalla's camp.

To win the second round in September, Megawati–Hasyim and Yudhoyono–Kalla had campaigned hard to woo the voters who initially voted for Wiranto–Wahid, Amien–Siswono, and Hamzah–Agum. Based on the results of the first round, the voters for these three pairs of candidates altogether numbered 47.3 million, consisting of about 26.3 million votes from Wiranto–Wahid, 17.4 million from Amien–Siswono, and 3.6 million from Hamzah–Agum. As shown in Figure 4.1, their supporters were concentrated in three densely populated provinces in Java comprising nearly 25 million — with the largest number from West Java, followed by East Java, and Central Java. The largest numbers for each of them also came from these three provinces, though the sequences were different. Wiranto–Wahid secured the largest number of votes from West Java, East Java, and Central Java; Amien–Siswono from West Java, Central Java, and East Java; while Hamzah–Agum from Central Java, West Java, and East Java. Furthermore, 62.2 per cent of the total voters of these three pairs were located in Java. The success of Megawati–Hasyim or Yudhoyono–Kalla would be determined by these votes in the September election. In other words, Java had been a very important battleground for the two grand finalists.

Table 4.1, which was based on the data collected on 2–9 September 2004, about two weeks before the second round, shows that Yudhoyono–Kalla had been preferred by the majority of all voters in the first round, except those who voted for Hamzah–Agum and particularly for Megawati–Hasyim. The pair retained almost all (98.8 per cent) of their first round voters. They could also bring most of

FIGURE 4.1
Number of Votes for Wiranto, Amien and Hamzah:
Presidential Elections 2004, Round 1

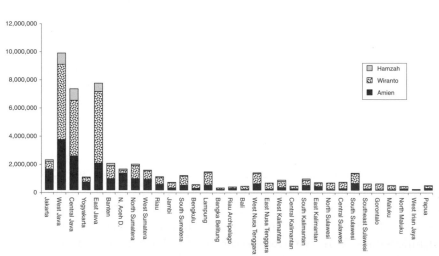

Source: Compiled from Table 3.3.

TABLE 4.1
Preference for Megawati–Hasyim and Yudhoyono–Kalla
(in Percentage): 2–9 September 2004

	Megawati–Hasyim	Yudhoyono–Kalla	Total
First Round			
Wiranto–Wahid	15.9	84.1	100.0
Megawati–Hasyim	91.9	8.1	100.0
Amien–Siswono	16.8	83.2	100.0
Yudhoyono–Kalla	1.2	98.8	100.0
Hamzah–Agum	55.6	44.4	100.0
Did not Vote	31.6	68.4	100.0
Secret	14.0	86.0	100.0

Note: Because the calculation of the percentages in the official results of the elections do not include those who did not vote and those with invalid votes, the percentages from the survey were recalculated by excluding those who did not give any answer during the survey.

Source: Compiled and calculated from IFES (2004*i*).

the Wiranto–Wahid and Amien–Siswono first round voters to their side. The pair also obtained the support of the majority of the first round Golput, those who did not vote, and those who did not want to reveal what they voted. Though not a very large vote, the pair received almost half of the first round voters for Hamzah–Agum. Efforts by the Megawati–Hasyim camp to woo Yudhoyono–Kalla's voters did not materialize. On the contrary, Megawati–Hasyim even lost their own voters — 8.1 per cent switched to Yudhoyono–Kalla.

These results could indicate that those who voted for Wiranto–Wahid and Amien–Siswono in the first round were mostly those who felt that the Yudhoyono–Kalla pair was the second best choice after their own candidates. Voters wanted "change" and they believed that the "change" could bring hope for improvement. Some of them might not even have considered Megawati–Hasyim, focussing instead on just two choices: Yudhoyono–Kalla or "Golput" ("do not vote").[1] The phenomenon of *asal bukan Mega* (anyone but Mega) revealed deep dissatisfaction of many voters with the government and might explain the success of Yudhoyono–Kalla in securing most of the votes in the second round.

It should be noted that mistakes in punching the ballot paper might have been fewer than in the first round. Facing the final round, the

Indonesian voters had to learn how to punch the ballot paper correctly as its size and layout was different from the one in the first round. The IFES survey conducted on 2–9 September 2004 shows that there was great awareness of the correct way to punch the ballot: 84 per cent of the respondents knew that they should punch the ballot only once for their preferred presidential/vice presidential pair. The invalid votes from the second round were more likely to indicate the Golput who purposely punched the ballot in the wrong way.

Furthermore, the survey also indicated that the voters in the first round were very likely to vote in the second round. Almost all (96 per cent) of those who voted for Wiranto–Wahid in the first round planned to vote in the second round. Wiranto's announcement of his support for Yudhoyono–Kalla might have boosted the participation of Wiranto–Wahid voters in the second round and raised the number of the votes for Yudhoyono–Kalla. This was a very significant contribution as Wiranto–Wahid voters were the largest among the defeated contenders.

On the other hand, there was a lower, though still high, likelihood, that Amien–Siswono voters (87 per cent) and Hamzah–Agum voters (83 per cent) wanted to vote again in the second round. Some of these voters might have considered whether to choose Yudhoyono–Kalla or Golput, and have refused to vote Megawati–Hasyim at all.

Finally, on 20 September 2004, Indonesian voters went to the polls to cast their ballot — and as revealed from the IFES post-September election survey (IFES 2004j), more voters had come to the polls with an intention to change Indonesia.

The September election, like the April and July elections, was smooth and peaceful. The post-September election survey indicates that almost all respondents (97 per cent) perceived that the second round had been fair and honest. Very few respondents (2 per cent) reported that they were offered money or other valuable rewards to vote for a particular pair and even fewer respondents (0.6 per cent) felt that they were pressured to choose a certain pair. This finding was similar to those on the parliamentary and first round of the presidential elections.

On Monday, 4 October 2004, the KPU officially announced the final results. There were 114,257,054 valid votes. From these valid votes, the retired general and his running mate who advocated "change for the better" won the second round of the presidential elections by securing 60.6 per cent of the votes, and Megawati–Hasyim, 39.4 per cent. Megawati–Hasyim did not challenge the results and Megawati announced on 5 October 2004 that she asked everybody to respect the results of the election. On 20 October 2004, Yudhoyono and Kalla were sworn in as the new Indonesian president and vice president respectively.

It can be mentioned here that, out of about 150 million eligible voters, around 33.9 million registered but did not vote.[2] If those eligible voters who did not register and those who voted but purposely made the votes invalid are included, the number of Golput would be larger than 33.9 million. In other words, seen from the overall eligible voters, rather than from the valid voters only, Golput comprised at least 22.6 per cent of all eligible voters after Yudhoyono–Kalla (around 46.2 per cent) and Megawati–Hasyim (around 30 per cent). Furthermore, the number of Golput in the second round was larger than in the first round, which was also larger than that in the parliamentary election. The rising number of Golput was probably due to the fact that some of the voters for the three defeated candidates in the first round might not feel that the two finalists were their choices at all.

Though winning the presidency, Yudhoyono–Kalla's popularity declined between the first and second rounds of the elections (see Table 4.2).[3] On the other hand, Megawati–Hasyim seemed to have been able

TABLE 4.2
Candidates' Popularity:
Early July – Late September 2004

Period	IFES		Period	LSI	
	Megawati–Hasyim	Yudhoyono–Kalla		Megawati–Hasyim	Yudhoyono–Kalla
7–14 July	26.7	73.3	17–19 July	25.3	74.7
7–14 August	31.2	68.8	23–25 August	33.2	66.8
2–9 September	32.2	67.8	10–12 September	34.8	65.2
			16 September	37.9	62.1
20 September	39.4	60.6	20 September	39.4	60.6
22–29 September	27.4	72.6			

Note: "20 September" refers to the official results of the second round. Because the calculation of the percentages in the official results of the elections do not include those who did not vote and those with invalid votes, the percentages from the survey were recalculated by excluding those who did not give any answer during the surveys.

Source: Compiled and recalculated from IFES (2004g), IFES (2004h) IFES (2004i), IFES (2004j), and LSI (no date).

to regain their popularity and yet it was too late for them to win the presidency-vice presidency. The three-day dialogue by the two pairs of candidates on TV one week before the polling day of the second round of the presidential elections may have helped slow down the decline of Yudhoyono–Kalla's popularity, especially in wooing the undecided voters in the last one week before the election. Yudhoyono, who had come across well in the mass media including TV, had again shown his superior ability in public relations. It can be noted here that 16 per cent of the respondents made their decisions in the last-one week (IFES October 2004) and that 89.7 per cent of the respondents learnt social and political issues, both regional and national, from television (LSI October 2004). Furthermore, the bombing in front of the Australian embassy in Jakarta on 10 September 2004 might not have had any effect on the voting — if it did, it might have been very little and might have reduced the drop in Yudhoyono–Kalla's popularity.

Interestingly, results from the post-September election survey by IFES show that Yudhoyono–Kalla's popularity had soared, as 72.6 per cent of the respondents were more likely to say that they voted for them in the one week after the election. However, a survey by the LSI on 7–8 December 2004 shows that the reversal seemed to be only temporary. The survey reveals that the popularity of Yudhoyono had started to decline especially in the urban communities. The impatience of the people and lack of political communication and public relations in managing many issues, particularly economic issues, may have caused the decline in Yudhoyono's popularity (LSI 2004b).

First and Second Round Performances

As discussed in Chapter 3, the results in the first round show that Yudhoyono–Kalla secured the first position in eighteen provinces — geographically arranged from the West to the East: Riau, Riau Archipelago, Jambi, South Sumatra, Lampung, Jakarta, Banten, West Java, Yogyakarta, East Java, Central Kalimantan, South Kalimantan, East Kalimantan, Central Sulawesi, South Sulawesi, Southeast Sulawesi, West Irian Jaya, and Papua. Though their victory varied from one province to another, ranging from 28.1 per cent in Yogyakarta to 64.2 per cent in South Sulawesi, the result was spectacular given that they were supported by only three small parties. Their popularity was not confined to some few provinces, but had been well spread throughout Indonesia.

FIGURE 4.2

**Votes for Yudhoyono and Megawati by Province:
Presidential Elections 2004, Round 1**

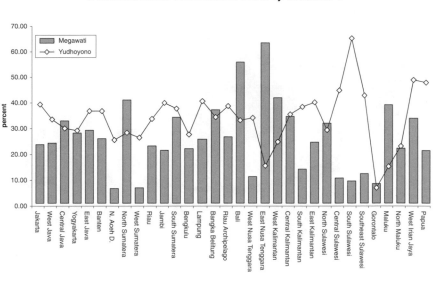

Source: Table 3.3.

Figure 4.2 shows that the Yudhoyono–Kalla victory in South
Sulawesi, Kalla's home province, was overwhelming, while Megawati–
Hasyim only obtained 8.5 per cent of the votes. Yudhoyono–Kalla's
great victory over Megawati–Hasyim was also the case in other provinces
in Sulawesi, namely Central Sulawesi and Southeast Sulawesi, though
the victories were not as large as in South Sulawesi. In Central Sulawesi,
43.7 per cent of the voters were for Yudhoyono–Kalla, in contrast to
only 9.7 per cent for Megawati–Hasyim. Central Sulawesi was similar
to Southeast Sulawesi, where Yudhoyono–Kalla earned 41.7 per cent of
the votes and Megawati–Hasyim only garnered 11.4 per cent. In Papua,
the easternmost province, Yudhoyono–Kalla's victory was also clear as
they obtained 46.7 per cent of the votes, against 20.3 per cent for
Megawati–Hasyim. Jusuf Kalla, the vice presidential candidate, might
have played an important role in this victory as he was a Sulawesi son
— born in South Sulawesi.

The Kalla factor seemed to have shown its stronger pulling power
in the second round. As seen in Figure 4.3, the Yudhoyono–Kalla pair

FIGURE 4.3
The Winning Candidates in the Second Round

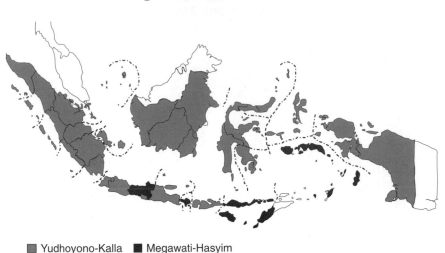

■ Yudhoyono-Kalla   ■ Megawati-Hasyim

gained their strong support not only in Sulawesi, but in most provinces in eastern Indonesia. They repeated their great success in South Sulawesi, where they earned 87.2 per cent of the votes. This was also the largest percentage of votes they secured in the second round. As in the first round, this pair obtained great success in Central Sulawesi (78.0 per cent) and Southeast Sulawesi (78.1 per cent). The pair continued the victory in West Nusa Tenggara, North Maluku, West Irian Jaya, and Papua. Megawati–Hasyim could not even take the leading positions over Yudhoyono–Kalla in North Sulawesi and Gorontalo, both in Sulawesi.

Yudhoyono–Kalla had also been successful in strengthening their victory in Nanggroe Aceh Darussalam, West Sumatra, West Nusa Tenggara, and Bengkulu. It should be noted that the 83.8 per cent of votes for Yudhoyono–Kalla in West Sumatra was the second largest after South Sulawesi. The fact that Yusuf Kalla's wife is a Minang[4] might have contributed to the success in West Sumatra.

The battle had been tough for Megawati–Hasyim. They lost in some provinces where they were expected to win. In the first round, Megawati–Hasyim won victory in six provinces, North Sumatra, Bangka Belitung, West Kalimantan, Central Java, Bali, and East Nusa Tenggara.

Their victory ranged from 31.8 per cent of the votes in Central Java to 62.3 per cent in East Nusa Tenggara. Megawati–Hasyim's support was far ahead in Bali, North Sumatra, East Nusa Tenggara and West Kalimantan, as the gaps between the two were significantly wide.

Nevertheless, in the second round Megawati–Hasyim could not maintain their victory in Bangka-Belitung and Central Java. The loss in Bangka-Belitung was not surprising as the PBB was the winning party in this province and also a strong supporter for Yudhoyono–Kalla during the presidential elections. Surprisingly, Megawati–Hasyim did not win in her party's stronghold province, Central Java. They gained 2.9 percentage points higher than Yudhoyono–Kalla in the first round but lost by 3.3 percentage points in the second round. More precisely, Yudhoyono–Kalla won a marginal victory with 51.7 per cent of the votes. This loss, though not great, may have indicated that the PDI-P, and Megawati, had serious trouble attracting voters.

Another province where Megawati–Hasyim could not retain their victory was North Sumatra. They won by 39.9 per cent over Yudhoyono–Kalla's 27.2 per cent in the first round but lost by about 5 percentage points to their contender in the second round. Furthermore, the victory in West Kalimantan, where the Muslims constituted only 57.6 per cent of the population, was very thin, Megawati–Hasyim managed to secure only 50.0 per cent of the vote. Though the number of Megawati–Hasyim votes in the second round was much larger than that in the first round, Yudhoyono–Kalla had obtained much more, implying that the voters for the defeated candidates had been more likely to vote for Yudhoyono–Kalla. Again, this result may show the loss of confidence in Megawati. It is interesting to note that Megawati–Hasyim took over Wiranto–Wahid's leading position in Maluku, where the number of Muslims and Christians were almost the same and there had been "religious" conflicts for several years, by securing 54.6 per cent of the votes.

Nevertheless, the Megawati–Hasyim pair was still able to show their power. They managed to remain the first winner in East Nusa Tenggara (71.9 per cent) and Bali (62.3 per cent), where about 90 per cent of the population are non-Muslims.

In short, Yudhoyono–Kalla had won in twenty-eight out of the thirty-two provinces, an increase from eighteen provinces in the first round, showing a much wider acceptance of the pair (see Figure 4.4). More detailed information on the number of votes each pair of candidates earned is shown in Table 4.3.

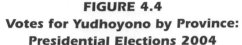

FIGURE 4.4
Votes for Yudhoyono by Province:
Presidential Elections 2004

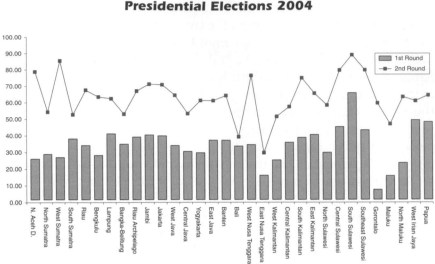

Source: Calculated from Table 4.3.

National Coalition's Poor Performance

Initially, there seemed to be a clear-cut strategy to win the September election. Yudhoyono–Kalla had repeatedly said that they would make a limited coalition, form a professional cabinet, rely on the principle of meritocracy — a cabinet consisting of more professionals and fewer politicians — and come closer to the people. On the other hand, Megawati–Hasyim had been busy building coalitions with other political leaders and planned to build a "rainbow" cabinet — consisting of mainly politicians. With the passage of time, nevertheless, both pairs started to adjust their strategies: Yudhoyono–Kalla also approached political leaders, while Megawati–Hasyim moved closer to the grassroots but continued the coalition approach.

Before the July election, Megawati–Hasyim (and her party, the PDI-P) had obtained support from the PDS. As mentioned in Chapter 1, after the first round, four parties (the PDI-P, PDS, Golkar, and PPP) officially declared the *Koalisi Kebangsaan* (National Coalition) on 19 August 2004. The declaration was also attended by the chairpersons of some small parties: the PBR, which supported Amien–Siswono in the first round, the PKPB, and PNI-Marhaenisme.[5] All together, these parties garnered 55.8 per cent in the parliamentary

TABLE 4.3
First and Second Round Results

	Megawati–Hasyim		Yudhoyono–Kalla	
	First	Second	First	Second
Nanggroe Aceh Darussalam	120,226	463,769	519,197	1,561,156
North Sumatra	2,233,777	2,530,065	1,523,612	2,808,212
West Sumatra	121,254	307,196	518,648	1,585,796
South Sumatra	1,127,608	1,652,302	1,241,095	1,719,016
Riau	460,328	680,707	677,761	1,309,245
Bengkulu	155,657	275,632	196,057	444,156
Lampung	896,581	1,407,236	1,430,729	2,165,778
Bangka-Belitung	179,777	221,715	165,657	233,454
Riau Archipelago	153,138	194,933	224,334	367,374
Jambi	273,925	402,542	520,145	917,952
Jakarta	1,235,272	1,587,902	2,083,950	3,559,297
West Java	5,095,705	7,825,251	7,100,175	13,186,776
Central Java	5,807,127	8,409,066	5,276,432	8,991,744
Yogyakarta	557,133	777,467	576,012	1,151,043
East Java	5,896,278	8,217,996	7,458,399	12,150,901
Banten	1,193,414	1,728,732	1,706,548	2,913,659
Bali	1,115,788	1,246,521	654,127	755,432
West Nusa Tenggara	223,204	522,411	715,838	1,563,494
East Nusa Tenggara	1,344,116	1,513,008	312,777	590,459
West Kalimantan	821,577	963,065	477,724	962,365
Central Kalimantan	296,335	374,546	303,123	474,839
South Kalimantan	211,881	399,528	600,156	1,096,637
East Kalimantan	337,458	482,247	558,900	856,365
North Sulawesi	389,135	523,903	355,436	686,688
Central Sulawesi	119,917	263,813	539,624	933,261
South Sulawesi	381,385	565,953	2,854,774	3,869,361
Southeast Sulawesi	108,905	202,705	398,544	721,792
Gorontalo	39,647	200,230	31,210	276,402
Maluku	269,611	374,437	100,748	311,269
North Maluku	98,459	170,975	102,353	277,077
Papua	202,295	380,091	465,424	642,869
West Irian Jaya	102,191	124,760	148,675	182,481
Total	31,569,104	44,990,704	39,838,184	69,266,350

Source: KPU.

election. If this coalition was effective, that is, if all voters from these parties had voted for Megawati–Hasyim, and voters from other parties had turned to Yudhoyono–Kalla, Megawati–Hasyim would have earned 55.7 per cent of the vote and become the president (see Table 4.4).

TABLE 4.4

National Coalition versus People's Coalition: Percentage of Votes based on Results of the Parliamentary Election

National Coalition		People's Coalition	
Golkar	21.58	PD	7.45
PDI-P	18.53	PKS	7.34
PPP	8.15	PBB	2.62
PBR	2.44	PKPI	1.26
PDS	2.13	PPDK	1.16
PKPB	2.11	PP	0.77
PNI-M	0.81	PPDI	0.75
Total	55.75	Total	21.35
		PKB	10.57
		PAN	6.44
		Total	38.36

Note: The remaining 5.89 per cent did not join either coalition.
          (See Chapters 1 and 2 for description of each party.)
Source: Compiled and calculated from <http://www.kpu.go.id>.

On the other hand, Yudhoyono–Kalla had also expanded their coalition. From only three parties supporting them before the first round (PD, PBB, and PKPI), they had received additional support from the PKS. These parties, which backed Yudhoyono–Kalla, declared the *Koalisi Kerakyatan* (People's Coalition) on 26 August 2004. This coalition was also supported by the PPDK, PP, and PPDI. The PKB and PAN officially declared to be independent, that they did not support either candidate, and yet they had unofficially supported Yudhoyono–Kalla.[6] In total, without the PKB and PAN, the People's Coalition would have secured only 21.4 per cent from the parliamentary elections, too small to win the presidency for Yudhoyono–Kalla. Even with the unofficial support from the PKB and PAN, the votes for Yudhoyono–Kalla would have been only 38.4 per cent, still less than that needed to win the presidency.

The real battle was not as smooth as the arithmetic calculation. There were internal conflicts within each party, and voters did not necessarily follow their political leaders. Golkar, the party with the largest votes in the parliamentary election, might have suffered the most from their own internal conflicts, between Akbar Tanjung's faction, which supported Megawati–Hasyim, and Fahmi Idris's faction, which backed Yudhoyono–Kalla. Several Golkar Party executives set up a forum, Golkar Party Reform Forum, on 31 August 2004 at Jakarta's Hotel

Hilton to bolster support for Yudhoyono and his running mate Kalla in the run-off presidential election. Kalla, himself a Golkar functionary, attended the declaration along with senior Golkar members Fahmi Idris, Marzuki Darusman, Burhanudin Napitupulu and Yorrys Raweyai, as well as hundreds of the party's supporters.

Table 4.5 shows that only 78 per cent of those who voted for the PDI-P in the parliamentary election preferred Megawati–Hasyim in the second round in contrast to almost 100 per cent for Yudhoyono–Kalla from those who voted for the PD in the parliamentary election. Megawati–Hasyim only received about 15 per cent of support from those who voted for Golkar in April, although this party was the largest party in the National Coalition. Among those who voted for the PPP, only 27 per cent would vote for Megawati–Hasyim in the pre-September election survey. Yet, the post-September election survey indicated that the support of the PPP voters had declined by about half. The Megawati–Hasyim pair was only successful in bringing PDS to the National Coalition, as this pair was able to attract 81 per cent of those who

TABLE 4.5
**Support for Presidential-Vice Presidential Candidates
by Party's Voters (in Percentages):
Pre- and Post-September Elections**

Party Voters	Megawati–Hasyim		Yudhoyono–Kalla		Not Known	
	Pre	Post	Pre	Post	Pre	Post
Golkar	14	16	79	82	7	2
PDI-P	78	78	18	20	4	2
PPP	27	13	62	84	12	3
PKB	28	16	69	84	3	0
PD	–	1	98	99	2	0
PKS	9	11	82	86	8	3
PAN	18	10	71	87	12	3
PBB	7	8	80	89	14	3
PBR	11	11	78	84	11	5
PDS	81	30	14	65	6	5
Secret	10	4	30	21	60	75
No response	27	0	40	36	34	64

Note: "not known" is a summation of "secret" and "no response";
        "Pre" refers to data collected on 2–9 September 2004;
        "Post" refers to data collected on 22–29 September 2004.
Source: IFES (2004*i*), Table 4 and IFES (2004*j*).

voted for PDS in April. Nevertheless, this is the data from the pre-September election survey. The post-September election survey reveals a drastic drop of the PDS voters to only 30 per cent. It is very interesting to further examine the very big drop of support for Megawati–Hasyim from the PPP, an Islamic party, and especially, the PDS, a party with Christians as its main constituent. They only garnered 11 per cent from those who voted for the PBR, another member of the coalition. Other declines in support for them were found in the PKB and PAN. Furthermore, Megawati–Hasyim obtained almost no support from the PD voters; only managed to get about 8 per cent from the PBB voters, and around 10 per cent from the PKS voters. In short, from this survey, it seemed that the National Coalition failed to support Megawati–Hasyim (see Table 4.5).

The competition to gain the Muslim voters was also keen, especially in wooing the voters from NU and Muhammadiyah. The support from the PKS and PAN had been very instrumental in boosting the Muhammadiyah support for Yudhoyono–Kalla, while the support from the PKB, particularly from Gus Dur, had also enhanced the number of the votes from NU for Yudhoyono–Kalla.

Background of the Supporters

Though it is important to know the background of the supporters who voted for their candidates, there is no such nationwide data available. The only available data was collected by the LSI on 16 September 2004, four days before the polling date. The LSI, as presented in Table 4.6, collected six socio-demographic variables, namely gender, age, urban–rural, education, religion, and ethnicity, as well as one variable measuring political stream, the NU-Muhammadiyah dichotomy. To strengthen the analysis, the results from a survey conducted by IFES from 2–9 September 2004 were also used, though the latter only provided information on age, urban–rural and education of the supporters.[7]

After excluding the respondents with no answers, 64.1 per cent of the Muslims preferred Yudhoyono–Kalla, compared to 35.9 per cent for Megawati–Hasyim. On the other hand, most (88.9 per cent) of the Buddhists chose Megawati–Hasyim, in contrast to 11.1 per cent for Yudhoyono–Kalla. As the majority of the Buddhists in Indonesia are ethnic Chinese, this preference for Megawati–Hasyim might show the strong inclination of the ethnic Chinese to back Megawati–Hasyim.

TABLE 4.6
Megawati–Hasyim's and Yudhoyono–Kalla's Supporters: Four Days before the Second Round

Background	With "no answer"			Without "no answer"		
	Megawati–Hasyim	Yudhoyono–Kalla	Total	Megawati–Hasyim	Yudhoyono–Kalla	Total
Age						
<20	28.9	67.5	96.4	30.0	70.0	100.0
20–29	31.7	58.9	90.6	35.0	65.0	100.0
30–39	37.1	51.5	88.6	41.9	58.1	100.0
40–49	35.3	49.2	84.5	41.8	58.2	100.0
>49	32.7	48.6	81.3	40.2	59.8	100.0
Gender						
Male	33.6	52.4	86.0	39.1	60.9	100.0
Female	34.9	52.9	87.8	39.7	60.3	100.0
Rural–Urban						
Rural	36.8	51.5	88.3	41.7	58.3	100.0
Urban	30.8	54.2	85.0	36.2	63.8	100.0
Education						
Elementary and lower	41.5	45.2	86.7	47.9	52.1	100.0
Junior Secondary	31.4	57.3	88.7	35.4	64.6	100.0
Senior Secondary	26.1	61.2	87.3	29.9	70.1	100.0
Tertiary or higher	14.4	68.0	82.4	17.5	82.5	100.0
Religion						
Islam	31.1	55.5	86.6	35.9	64.1	100.0
Christianity	55.8	34.2	90.0	62.0	38.0	100.0
Hinduism	60.0	28.9	88.9	67.5	32.5	100.0
Buddhism	72.7	9.1	81.8	88.9	11.1	100.0
Ethnicity						
Javanese	33.6	51.3	84.9	39.6	60.4	100.0
Sundanese	39.9	49.3	89.2	44.7	55.3	100.0
Malay	30.7	56.7	87.4	35.1	64.9	100.0
Madurese	40.3	58.2	98.5	40.9	59.1	100.0
Batak	36.6	45.5	82.1	44.6	55.4	100.0
Others	31.9	55.9	87.8	36.3	63.7	100.0
NU-Muhammadiyah						
NU	35.6	55.0	90.6	39.3	60.7	100.0
Muhammadiyah	19.6	69.6	89.2	22.0	78.0	100.0

Source: Compiled and calculated from LSI (no date).

This pair was also popular among the Christians, as 62.0 per cent of the Christian respondents chose them. A large percentage of the Hindus (67.5 per cent) gave their voice to Megawati–Hasyim, and 32.5 per cent supported Yudhoyono–Kalla. Megawati–Hasyim was actually expected to gain more among the Hindus because Bali was one of Megawati's party strongholds and the Hindus residing in Bali, as enumerated in the 2000 population census, accounted for 75.4 per cent of the total Hindus in Indonesia. However, this result does not necessarily mean that Megawati–Hasyim supporters were dominated by the non-Muslims — the number of Muslims in Indonesia was so much larger than that of the non-Muslims. Rather, the result may indicate that Megawati–Hasyim's supporters were more pluralistic in terms of religious followers than those for Yudhoyono–Kalla.

Yudhoyono–Kalla was more attractive to the younger ones, the first-time voters, than Megawati–Hasyim. As shown in Table 4.6, about 70 per cent of those aged less than 20 years old would choose them and about 65 per cent of the older ones, 20–29 years old, would do so. Yudhoyono's presence and his popular song sung at the *Akademi Fantasi Indosiar* (an Indonesian version of "American Idol"), which has become very popular among Indonesian TV watchers, may have helped to boost Yudhoyono's popularity among the young voters. Among the older ones, Yudhoyono and Kalla were favoured by around 58 per cent.

The IFES survey also found a similar finding. Therefore, although the pair of Yudhoyono–Kalla was more likely to be preferred in all age groups, the support was stronger from the younger the age group. Among those under 25 years old, 68 per cent would support Yudhoyono–Kalla. The percentage decreased to 46 per cent among those who were older than 54 years old. In contrast, the support for Megawati–Hasyim increased as the age of the supporters increased. The support for Megawati–Hasyim was 25 per cent among those aged below 25 years and increased to 39 per cent among those aged above 54 years.

Both surveys found that the higher the education of the respondents, the more likely did they choose Yudhoyono–Kalla. Yudhoyono had also been perceived as "a thinking general" — indeed, he earned his doctoral degree just two days before the second round of the presidential elections.

The Yudhoyono–Kalla campaign slogan "Together We Can (*Bersama Kita Bisa*)" was primarily targetted at the middle class in urban areas. Their top priorities of improving security and the investment climate were also directed to win the hearts of these people, although all these campaign slogans also resonated with rural voters. The LSI survey showed that they had garnered greater support among urban respondents (63.8 per cent), though the difference with the support from rural respondents was only 5.5 percentage points. Earlier surveys by the IFES also show the same pattern but the difference was smaller (63 per cent) among urban respondents and 60 per cent among rural ones. The LSI survey also showed that there was no important difference in the support from male and female respondents.

Table 4.6 indicates some differences in preferences among different ethnic groups, but the difference was not large — the preference ranged only within 10 percentage points. The strongest support for Yudhoyono–Kalla came from the Malay (64.9 per cent), and the weakest one from the Sundanese (55.3 per cent). After the Malay, the second strongest support came from "other ethnic groups" (63.7 per cent), probably reflecting many ethnic groups in eastern Indonesia, enticed by the presence of Kalla as his vice presidential candidate. However, the support from the Javanese, which Yudhoyono belongs to, was only the third largest for this pair. It is interesting that the two largest ethnic groups supporting Megawati–Hasyim were the Sundanese and Batak — almost half of the Sundanese and Batak would vote for Megawati–Hasyim. The next two largest ethnic groups were the Madurese (40.9 per cent) and Javanese (39.6 per cent). In summary Yudhoyono–Kalla acquired more votes than Megawati–Hasyim in all categories, except among non-Muslims.

Megawati's choice of Hasyim Muzadi, the leader of the NU, the country's largest Muslim group, should have given her a fair chance to win the presidential race. However, as shown in Table 4.6, Megawati–Hasyim was unsuccessful in gaining much support from the NU, but the Yudhoyono–Kalla team was able to garner greater support from both Muhammadiyah (78 per cent) and NU (60.7 per cent) — the two largest Islamic social organizations in Indonesia.

Personality versus Policy

Table 4.7 indicates that the percentage of those who considered personality as more important remained almost the same, 38 per cent in August and 39 per cent in September. On the other hand, there had been a little increase in those who considered policy as more important than personality. The percentage rose from 23 per cent in August to 26 per cent in September, but still lower than the percentages citing

TABLE 4.7

Personality versus Policy: Pre- and Post-September elections

Important considerations	Pre-September election		Post-September election
	August	September	
Policy	23	26	28
Personality	38	39	36
Equal	37	34	35
No answer	2	2	2
Total	100	101	101

Note: August refers to the results of IFES survey from 7 to 14 August 2004; September refers to the results of IFES survey from 2 to 9 September 2004; Post-election refers to the results of IFES survey from 22 to 29 September 2004.
Source: Compiled from IFES (2004*h*), IFES (2004*i*) and IFES (2004*j*).

personality as the more important consideration. IFES (September 2004) also mentioned that the pattern shown in the table did not change much when the supporters of Megawati–Hasyim were analysed separately from those of Yudhoyono–Kalla. Furthermore, the percentage of those who considered personality as the more important consideration only slightly declined to 36 per cent in the post–September election survey conducted on 22–29 September. Consistently, the percentage of those who considered policy as more important increased only a little to 28 per cent. In other words, people had put more weight on personality than policies when they chose their president, a phenomenon which had been consistently found since the first round of the presidential elections.

Indonesians who intended to vote either for Megawati–Hasyim or Yudhoyono–Kalla said that "honesty and good personality" was the most important consideration for their choice. As shown in Table 4.8, in August IFES survey, 41 per cent of the respondents mentioned "honesty and good personality" as the most frequently cited consideration to choose a president. The percentage declined to 35 per cent in September because the respondents gave slightly more weight to other considerations such as "Having concern about people" and "Firmness and capacity to maintain stability". "Having concern about

TABLE 4.8
Criteria for a President

Criteria	August		September	
	%	Rank	%	Rank
Honesty and good personality	41	1	35	1
Having concern about people	18	2	20	2
Firmness and capacity to maintain stability	11	4	15	3
Capacity to lead the country	16	3	11	4
Capacity to bring economic recovery	7	6	9	5–6
Others	8	5	9	5–6
Total	101*		99*	

Note: August refers to the results from IFES survey on 7 to 14 August 2004;   September refers to the results from IFES survey on 2 to 9 September 2004.
  * The total does not sum up to 100 due to rounding the numbers up.
Source: Compiled from IFES (2004*h*) and IFES (2004*i*).

people" remained the second criterion in both surveys. "Capacity" to maintain stability, to lead the country, and to bring economic recovery were the next criteria — meaning that "capacity" was a less important consideration to choose a president.

The September survey shows that 68 per cent of the respondents who intended to vote for Yudhoyono–Kalla mentioned personality, leadership and firmness as their important considerations. The percentage was larger than 51 per cent, who intended to vote for Megawati–Hasyim. Twenty-four per cent of respondents intending to vote for Megawati–Hasyim were more likely to say that they want someone who cares for the common people than those intending to vote for Yudhoyono–Kalla (17 per cent).

With regard to a candidate's stance on policy issues, the economic ones were more frequently mentioned than those such as security and social issues. Keeping prices low, reducing corruption, and creating jobs were the three economic issues frequently raised by the respondents. About 80 per cent of the respondents mentioned one of these three issues in August and September. "Improving security" was mentioned by only 6 per cent of the respondents in August and 7 per cent in September; while "maintaining territorial integrity of Indonesia" was considered important by 6 per cent of the respondents in August and

5 per cent in September. "Fighting terrorism" was cited by even much smaller percentages, only 1.2 per cent in August and 0.5 per cent in September (see Table 4.9).

The survey also found that the respondents believed that Yudhoyono–Kalla would be able to better implement policies on each of the above issues. However, Yudhoyono–Kalla's greatest superiority over Megawati–Hasyim, as perceived by the respondents, was in the area of security. Yudhoyono's military background may have contributed to this image.

The relatively more important weight on personality than substantive issues in choosing a president is not really surprising. The programmes introduced by both Megawati–Hasyim and Yudhoyono–Kalla were very similar in substance. During the presidential election campaign, candidates gave many promises, from the fields of law, the economy, education, to governance. The research team of *Kompas* compiled a series of promises put forward by five pairs of candidates based on their statements made during their campaigns between 19 April and 15 June 2004. There were more similarities than differences in these promises. However, for illustration purposes, only those of the Megawati–Hasyim and Yudhoyono–Kalla teams are shown (see Table 4.10).

TABLE 4.9
Important Policy Issues

	August		September	
	%	Rank	%	Rank
Keeping prices low	25	3	30	1
Reducing corruption	29	1	28	2
Creating jobs	26	2	21	3
Improving security	6	4–5	7	4
Maintaining territorial integrity of Indonesia	6	4–5	5	5–6
Improving quality of education	4	6	5	5–6
Fighting terrorism	1.2	7	0.5	8–9
Reducing environment degradation	0.4	9	0.5	8–9
Improving health care	0.5	8	1.4	7
Total	98.1		98.4	

Note: August refers to the results from the IFES survey on 7 to 14 August 2004; September refers to the results from the IFES survey on 2 to 9 September 2004.
Source: Compiled from IFES (2004*h*) and IFES (2004*i*).

TABLE 4.10
Programmes and Promises

Field	Megawati–Hasyim	Yudhoyono–Kalla
Law	To take tactical and strategic steps to combat corruption; to punish drug traffickers very heavily.	To establish law and order, to combat KKN and to review all policies and regulations which hindered the freedom of religious life.
Economy	To empower cooperatives, to encourage SME activities and cooperatives, to offer subsidies for fertilizers, to offer SME credit without collateral.	To increase per capita income to US$1,731 in 2009, to build economic infrastructure in east Indonesia, to stabilize prices of commodities.
Education	To employ 100,000 school teachers per year, to increase the number of scholarships, to produce a fair distribution of education, to eliminate tax on text books, to provide free education for orphans.	To enhance the quality of education, to improve infrastructure for public education and *pesantren* (Islamic boarding school), to provide free education for those who cannot afford it.
Social Issues	To reduce the percentage of the poor and the unemployed, to create more jobs, to protect minority groups.	To reduce poverty, to reduce unemployment, to create jobs, to pay attention to the labourers.
Government	Cabinet ministers should be loyal to the state and national leaders, be capable and clean, to establish a clean and just government.	To establish limited coalition cabinet, to provide TNI/Police with a special budget to resolve conflicts, to sign special autonomy law for Papua.
Others	To continue the construction of the Trans-Kalimantan bridge, to build national mentality.	Within 100 days president will not travel overseas, the president will make regular communications with the press once or twice a month.

Source: Kompas (2004*c*) "Capres-capres Sudah Berjanji, Rakyat Menunggu Bukti", p. 8.

The promises of the two pairs of candidates were quite similar in terms of their economic policy, except that Megawati–Hasyim stressed the SMEs and cooperatives, while Yudhoyono–Kalla were more concerned with the macroeconomics. On the issue of corruption, both pairs of candidates promised that they would combat corruption. The only difference was on the issue of the minorities, and religion. Megawati–Hasyim did not say much about religion, but they talked about the protection of the minorities. Yudhoyono–Kalla on the other hand did talk about freedom of religious life and improvement of education in the *pesantren*. Unlike the Megawati–Hasyim team, the Yudhoyono–Kalla team proposed that the TNI/Police be given a special budget for their operation to resolve regional conflicts.

Concluding Remarks

Perubahan (change) has been the catchword. The Yudhoyono–Kalla team was elected on the expectation of change for a better Indonesia. In *Indonesia 2004–2009: Vision for Change* (Brighten Press), Yudhoyono said:

> ... when speaking of "change", I must specify that I am talking about change for the better. Change itself is easy. But change for the sake of changing is useless. And no one wants to change for the worse....

The Yudhoyono–Kalla pair was a magnet especially among the young and educated voters. The Megawati–Hasyim pair was able to perform well among non-Muslims, in particular the Buddhists as this may reflect a large support of the ethnic Chinese for this pair. In terms of ethnicity, the Yudhoyono–Kalla pair was most popular among the Malay and "others" (meaning other than Javanese, Sundanese, Malay, Madurese, and Batak), while the Megawati–Hasyim pair had the best support among the Sundanese and Batak. In wooing the Muslims, the Yudhoyono–Kalla team was able to gain the majority support from both the NU and Muhammadiyah.

In the early part of the campaigning, the two camps seemed to have clear-cut strategies. On the one hand, the Megawati–Hasyim camp depended mostly on the National Coalition, getting support from party leaders; on the other hand, the Yudhoyono–Kalla camp relied strongly on the support from the grassroots, optimizing Yudhoyono's rising personal popularity. However, as the battle went on, the Megawati–Hasyim camp also approached the grassroots and the Yudhoyono–Kalla camp attempted to establish a wider coalition. Indeed, the People's Coalition was formed to support Yudhoyono–Kalla.

During the second round of the presidential elections, voters seemed to have identified the economy as the most important issue to be handled by the new president — this issue was mentioned by about 80 per cent of the respondents in a survey conducted in September, before the second round. On the other hand, security was much less important, mentioned by only about 7 per cent of the respondents. The fact that finally Yudhoyono–Kalla, rather than Megawati–Hasyim, won the elections indicates that voters had believed that the Yudhoyono–Kalla pair would be better able to solve economic issues than the Megawati–Hasyim pair.

Notes

1. See the discussion on "Golput" in Chapter 1.
2. As mentioned in Chapter 1, 150 million is our conservative estimate. The 33.9 million is quoted from KPU "Jumlah Riil yang Tak Menggunakan Hak Pilih Tidak Sampai 33.981.479 Orang", Wednesday, 6 October 2004.
3. Table 4.2 shows two data sets, one from the IFES and another from the LSI. Both data sets consistently reveal the declining popularity of Yudhoyono–Kalla. To be consistent with the official results of the elections which do not include those who did not vote and did not give any answer, the IFES and LSI results were recalculated by excluding those who did not give any answer in the IFES and LSI surveys.
4. Jusuf Kalla's wife, Mufidah, was born in Padang on 12 February 1943 and is the daughter of a teacher and an activist of the Muhammadiyah organization. <http://www.sbyudhoyono.com/VPProfile.aspx>.
5. As described in Chapter 1, PKPB is a split from Golkar, while PNI Marhaenism is a split from the PDI-P.
6. As an illustration, Yenny Wahid, the daughter of Gus Dur, was active in the campaign team of Yudhoyono–Kalla.
7. We believe that these two data sets (collected by the LSI and the IFES) may reflect the profile of the voters on polling day.

5

Peaceful Transition Towards Democracy

The 2004 elections were over. For the first time in history, Indonesia had a president who was directly elected by the people. The inauguration of President Susilo Bambang Yudhoyono and Vice President Jusuf Kalla took place on 20 October 2004 at the legislature complex in Jakarta. Their inauguration marked a major step forward in Indonesia's democratic transition. It was the first time that foreign leaders had witnessed the swearing in of a new Indonesian president and vice president. They included Singapore Prime Minister Lee Hsien Loong, Malaysian Prime Minister Abdullah Badawi, and Australian Prime Minister John Howard.

This chapter deals with the significance of the 2004 elections as a peaceful path towards democracy, the new president and his cabinet, and some discussions on what the Yudhoyono–Kalla's administration achieved during their first hundred days in power.

Significance of the 2004 Elections

This was the third democratic election and the first direct presidential election in Indonesia's history. The 2004 elections were a victory for Indonesia's democracy as they were conducted peacefully. Megawati was a responsible leader. She did not use dirty tactics in order to win the elections nor did she encourage violence to maintain power. She allowed the elections to proceed democratically and accepted the results, although she refused to attend the transfer of power ceremony, claiming that there was no such regulation in place. Her acceptance of the results prevented upheaval and bloodshed. One can argue that she made a significant contribution in the history of Indonesian democracy. She played a role as a transitional leader who consolidated the democratic process of the democratic elections, following the peaceful stepping down of B.J. Habibie and Gus Dur.

Observers and analysts, both in and outside Indonesia, had been worried about the possible disruption of, or violence during the 2004 elections. The months prior to the second round of the presidential elections had been predicted to be more tense and hence more likely to have clashes. The announcement of the second-round results could have been followed by strong protests and violence. Bombs could have been exploded to disturb the elections, but it did not happen. It appears that the Indonesian people were satisfied with the implementation of the elections. According to the surveys conducted by IFES (IFES 2004j), 86 per cent of the respondents expressed that the April 2004 election was "fair and honest". The percentage rose to 93 per cent for the July election and reached 97 per cent for the September election. There were also very few indications of vote buying and intimidation during the three elections (April, July and September 2004).

Differences in opinion and exchange of critiques were abundant, but this could be seen as a sign of a rising democracy in Indonesia. All political parties accepted the results of the elections; voters of the defeated candidates were not happy but they did not cause any instability to the country. A post-September election survey conducted on 2–4 October 2004 (LSI 2004j) found that 61.9 per cent of the respondents were satisfied or very satisfied with the current trend of democracy in Indonesia.

Nevertheless, the democratic political culture of Indonesia is still new and fragile, and needs to be promoted further. The 2004 elections brought Indonesians to the gate of democracy. The peaceful and successful elections of 2004 will be recorded in Indonesian history as a possible model but this model should not be taken for granted. Whether this is a viable model for Indonesia in the future will depend on the success or failure of the government policy and further development of radical Islam in the country.

A free and fair general election is the basis of a democratic system, which is in turn based on the political party system. In other words, it is impossible to have a democratic system without political parties.

After the fall of Soeharto, there was a revival of political parties which led to the development of democracy in Indonesia.

Indeed, the Indonesian political system has undergone significant change since Indonesia's independence, but it is incorrect to argue that there was only change without continuity. The authoritarian system has indeed been replaced by a democratic system but primordial sentiments and traditional outlooks have not been completely eradicated. The division of the Indonesian political culture, secular nationalism and Islamic nationalism, may have continued as reflected in Indonesian political parties. In both 1999 and 2004 elections, secular nationalist parties gained the majority votes but Islamic parties secured impressive votes. There was a tendency that Islamic parties/organizations in the 1999 election started to adopt the *Pancasila* ideology as the party basis, the best examples being the NU-based PKB and the Muhammadiyah-based PAN. However, many Muslims and non-Muslims still perceive the PKB and PAN as "Islamic parties". In general the political parties can still be divided into two political streams: secularist and Islamist, though the border between the two, especially in the PKB and PAN, may have been blurred.

The development of Islamic parties is particularly interesting. Soon after the fall of Soeharto, there was fragmentation of Islamic parties, but gradually a re-consolidation process took place. During the 2004 elections, there were only five Islamic parties instead of eighteen, representing three types of Islam: Traditionalist Islam (PPP, PBR and PPNUI), Modernist Islam (PBB) and New Generation Islam (PKS).[1] In addition, the dichotomy between Java and the Outer Islands has often been reflected in political parties. The PDI-P, for instance, is more a Java-based party. However, this division is not as strong as in the 1955 election, due to the interaction between Java and the Outer Islands in the last four decades which resulted in the emergence of more Indonesian communities.

President Yudhoyono

Yudhoyono was little known in the early 2004 but he then zoomed to popularity after late March 2004. He won the first and second rounds of the direct presidential elections and was eventually elected as the sixth Indonesian president. He is aware of the myriad problems that Indonesia faces and the difficulty in achieving the promises that he made during the campaign. People who were disappointed with the then President Megawati and voted for Yudhoyono wanted to see a change, if not a miracle, under the new president. He knows that people have a very high expectation of him. Not surprisingly, during his swearing-in as the sixth president of Indonesia, he told the people that they should not have too high an expectation of him.

The rise of Yudhoyono poses a number of interesting questions, raised even before and during the presidential campaigns — whether an ex-general who became a politician would reverse Indonesian politics back to the New Order era, whether Yudhoyono-Kalla would also make Indonesia more Islamic and eventually declare the *syari'ah* law as the law of the land. Before answering the questions, it is useful to recapture a brief biography of the new, first directly elected, president.

He was born into a modest family in Tremas (Pacitan, East Java) fifty-six years ago. His father, Soekotjo, was a low ranking army officer while his mother, Habibah, was the daughter of a founder of the Tremas Pesantren (Islamic Boarding School).[2] Nevertheless, Yudhoyono was not sent to the *pesantren* but to the state school in his hometown where he spent twelve years for both his primary and secondary education. This education and the traditional Javanese cultural environment influenced his later development. According to *Kompas*, he liked to read comics and wayang stories. It is also worth noting that he lived with his uncle who was a village head at Pacitan rather than with his parents. From his early student days, Yudhoyono was a star performer in whatever he did. He was hard working, intelligent, always a leader and number one in his class. As a student, he was known to have acquired a strong reading habit that remains until today.

His joining the military was not a coincidence. When he was in Primary 5, he visited the Akabri (Indonesian armed forces academy) in Magelang with his school classmates which left a strong impression on his young mind. This visit and his father's profession might have influenced his decision to join the Akabri.[3]

After high school graduation Yudhoyono successfully applied to the Akabri where he spent three years. He graduated as the top student in his batch in 1973. Upon graduation, he was assigned to be the assistant to General Sarwo Edhie Wibowo, then governor of the Akabri (1973–76). Sarwo Edhie was chief of the Army Para-Commando Regiment (RPKAD) during the 1965 coup and was an important military figure in the Soeharto era.[4] In 1976, Yudhoyono married one of Sarwo Edhie's daughters, Kristiani Herrawati, who was then a medical student at the Indonesian Christian University (UKI).

Partly due to his command of English, Yudhoyono was selected to go to the United States for advanced military training in Fort Banning, Georgia. He went again between 1982–83. He also had shorter training stints in Belgium and Germany. In 1991 he returned to the United States to study at the Webster University at Missouri, where he obtained an M.A. degree. He was often sent overseas as a member of Indonesia's representatives, and in 1995 he became the head of the United Nations Observers in Bosnia.

In July 1996, during the attack on the PDI-Megawati headquarters, Yudhoyono was chief of staff of the Jakarta Military Region. The incident was a point of debate during the 2004 Presidential Election Campaign. In 1996 the PDI split into two and the Megawati-led PDI was defeated by the military-sponsored PDI in the congress. The Jakarta PDI headquarters, occupied by the Megawati faction, was to be evacuated for the "new" leadership. However, the Megawati faction refused, leading to forced evacuation by the para-military group, resulting in many casualties. Yudhoyono was accused of being involved but he continued to deny it.

In 1998 Yudhoyono was appointed as the Indonesian armed forces' Kasospol (Chief of Social and Political Section) in charge of the political and social roles of the Indonesian military. In fact, in the last few years before the fall of Soeharto, the military was constantly under criticism. Yudhoyono, as the Kasospol, led a team to reform the Indonesian Armed Forces. His exposure to Western ideas may have had an impact here. The concept of *Dwi Fungsi* or Dual Function, which guaranteed the military's role in politics during the Soeharto era, was modified to that of *Peran Abri*, which means simply "the military role".[5] This was an astute piece of compromise, whereby the military no longer involves itself with the day-to-day politics but does not abandon completely *Dwi Fungsi* either. Nevertheless, the new doctrine also restricts the military's role so that it will not dominate politics. The Kasospol was eliminated in the following year by General Wiranto, the commander in chief of the Indonesian Armed Forces, to de-emphasize the non-security role of the Indonesian military.

Yudhoyono began to emerge as a major figure during the final days of Soeharto's rule. But after the fall of Soeharto, Habibie did not have him in his cabinet. Gus Dur appointed him as his mines and energy minister and a year later, as his chief security minister to replace General Wiranto, who was sacked. However, when Gus Dur was impeached by the People's Consultative Assembly, Yudhoyono was instructed by Gus Dur to declare martial law. Yudhoyono declined to follow the instruction, resulting in his dismissal. One can argue that he was able to see the general trends in Indonesian politics, showing his skills as a future politician.

When Megawati took over from Gus Dur, the position of the vice president was vacant. Yudhoyono contested the vice presidential election but lost to Hamzah Haz and Akbar Tanjung in the first round. Although he failed in the vice presidential contest, Yudhoyono was again appointed to serve as the coordinating minister of politics and security in her cabinet. Nevertheless, soon after the contest, a group of Yudhoyono's supporters, upon his suggestion, began to organize a political party, later known as the Partai Demokrat (PD, Democrat Party), which was used as his power base during the 2004 elections.

The PD was established on 9 September 2002, which is the birthday of Yudhoyono. It was done deliberately to show the party's connection with Yudhoyono. Although he did not hold any position in the PD, his wife, Kristiani, was one of the deputy chairpersons. Kristiani was his eyes and ears in the party as well as in politics in general. Many leaders of the PD were professionals and university intellectuals. The chairman of the party, Subur Budhisantoso, was a professor in the Department of Anthropology at the University of Indonesia. Understandably, Yudhoyono eventually came into conflict with Megawati when the PD contested the 2004 elections and proposed him as its presidential candidate. It was reported that Yudhoyono was excluded from the cabinet meeting after 1 March 2004. His exclusion from the cabinet resulted in his resignation and gained a lot of votes for Yudhoyono's PD party.

Following the party's success in the parliamentary elections in April 2004, Yudhoyono was officially nominated by the PD to be its presidential candidate. Yudhoyono also selected Jusuf Kalla, a Muslim businessman of Buginese origin, as his vice presidential candidate and formed an alliance with a small Islamic party, the Partai Bulan Bintang (PBB) led by Yusril Izha Mahendra. Because of his association with Jusuf Kalla who was seen to be anti-Christian and anti-Chinese, together with the PBB, which fought for a state based on the Islamic *syari'ah* law, Yudhoyono was under attack. He was accused of attempting to change Indonesia from the *Pancasila* state to an Islamic state. This voice became louder after the Partai Keadilan Sejahtera (PKS, Indonesian Prosperous Justice Party), an Islamic party, which won 7.3 per cent of the votes in the April election, threw its support behind Yudhoyono.

However, his rivals in the Islamic camp also accused him of being pro-Christian and anti-Islam. They branded him as a Muslim who was not pious and spread rumours that his wife, Kristiani, was a Christian. However, Yudhoyono commented that he favoured pluralism for Indonesia and would introduce a fair and just policy for all ethnic and religious groups. There was also an issue of "military versus civilian". Many people who suffered under the military rule in the New Order were afraid that military rule would return through retired generals if one of them was elected president of Indonesia. Nevertheless, Yudhoyono, a retired general who served in Soeharto's administration, maintained that he was a democrat and the post-Soeharto Indonesia could no longer introduce a military system.

During the first round of the presidential elections on 5 July 2004, Yudhoyono–Kalla occupied the number one position but he only secured 33.6 per cent of the votes while the Megawati–Hasyim won 26.6 per cent of the total votes. Since no one was able to gain 50 per cent of the vote, the second round was conducted on 20 September 2004. Most of the observers believed that the competition was keen and the margin of victory of the presidential candidate would be narrow. However, when the results were announced, Yudhoyono–Kalla gained 61.2 per cent while Megawati–Hasyim only gained 38.8 per cent, indicating that Yudhoyono secured much greater support in this first direct presidential election in the history of Indonesia. Why did Yudhoyono–Kalla win?

One of the reasons was the growing dissatisfaction with the Megawati administration. People wanted change for the better, in the social and security fields, and more importantly in the economy. Since the presidential elections had something to do with personality and images, Yudhoyono was able to impress the voters that he was a better and more capable candidate than Megawati. People had very high expectations of Yudhoyono.

From the above brief biography, it is clear that Yudhoyono has more of a "secular nationalist" orientation than that of "Islamic nationalist". It is unlikely that he would endorse the formation of an Islamic state, declaring *syari'ah* law as the law of the land. As an ex-military man and also a nationalist, he is concerned with Indonesian unity and has no tolerance for separatist movements. He is prepared to compromise provided that the blueprint of a unified Indonesia is not challenged. No doubt he has a strong military background, but he has gradually transformed himself into a politician, adopting the rules of the political game. His military background gives him the military connection but he has accepted the democratic system as the basis for the rules of the game. Like most politicians, he made compromises in order to come to power and subsequently, to rule Indonesia.

The "United Indonesia Cabinet":
A Reflection of Political Reality?

The compromises that Yudhoyono had to make were reflected in the cabinet line-up. Initially, Yudhoyono wanted to have a "professional" cabinet but apparently it was impossible. Yudhoyono had to respond to pressure from his political allies and beyond. He also needed to consider his own political survival. The selection process for the new cabinet members was lengthy. It started on 15 October and was supposed to have been completed on 19 October 2004 and announced on 20 October. However, the announcement was only made late in the night of 20 October after hard negotiations.

The so-called "United Indonesia (*Indonesia Bersatu*)" cabinet members were sworn in on 21 October 2004 at the State Palace (Kompas 2004*e*). The new thirty-six-member cabinet, which is larger than Megawati's thirty-three-member cabinet, includes 3 coordinating ministers (politics and security, economy, and welfare), 18 ministers in charge of ministries, 12 ministers with no ministries and 3 positions which are equivalent to ministers (attorney general, state secretary and chairperson of the National Development Planning Agency). The increased number was a result of a split of the ministry of trade and industry into two, a creation of the minister for public housing and minister of the arts, culture and sport. See Table 5.1 for the structure of the cabinet and the names of the persons filling the posts.

There were many interpretations on the cabinet; some were critical but others were complimentary. *Jakarta Post* (23 October 2004), for instance, argued that this is a fresh break, an attempt to reflect the country's diversity — a smart move by the new president. The members of the cabinet were recruited from business people, academics, bureaucrats, former ministers, retired military and police officers, and politicians. One third of the members are from the Outer Islands, four are non-Muslims, and four, as promised in the Yudhoyono–Kalla campaign, are women. During the campaign, Yudhoyono–Kalla also promised to include ethnic Chinese in the cabinet and this is shown in the appointment of Mari E. Pangestu as the trade minister.

TABLE 5.1
United Indonesia Cabinet, 2004

No.	Name	Position
1	Widodo A.S.	Coordinating Minister for Political, Legal and Security Affairs
2	Aburizal Bakrie	Coordinating Minister for the Economy
3	Alwi Shihab	Coordinating Minister for People's Welfare
4	Yusril Ihza Mahendra	Menteri Sekretaris Negara
5	Moh. Ma'ruf	Minister of Home Affairs
6	Nur Hassan Wirajuda	Minister of Foreign Affairs
7	Juwono Sudarsono	Minister of Defence
8	Hamid Awaluddin	Minister of Justice and Human Rights
9	Jusuf Anwar	Minister of Finance
10	Purnomo Yusgiantoro	Minister of Energy and Natural Resources
11	Andung Nitimiharja	Minister of Industry
12	Mari Elka Pangestu	Minister of Trade
13	Anton Apriyantono	Minister of Agriculture
14	M.S. Kaban	Minister of Forestry
15	Hatta Radjasa	Minister of Transportation and Communication
16	Freddy Numberi	Minister of Maritime Affairs and Fisheries
17	Fahmi Idris	Minister of Manpower and Transmigration
18	Djoko Kirmanto	Minister of Public Works
19	Fadilah Supari	Minister of Health
20	Bambang Sudibyo	Minister of Education

continued on next page

TABLE 5.1 – cont'd

No.	Name	Position
21	Bachtiar Chamsyah	Minister of Social Services
22	M. Maftuh Basyuni	Minister of Religious Affairs
23	Jero Wacik	State Minister of Culture and Tourism
24	Kusmayanto Kadiman	State Minister for Research and Technology
25	Suryadharma Ali	State Minister for Cooperatives and Small and Medium Enterprises
26	Rachmat Witoelar	State Minister of Environment
27	Meutia Farida Hatta Swasono	State Minister for Women Empowerment
28	Taufik Effendi	State Minister for Administrative Reform
29	Saifullah Yusuf	State Minister for Acceleration of Development in Backward Regions
30	Sri Mulyani Indrawati	Chairperson of the National Development Planning Agency (Bappenas)
31	Sugiharto	State Minister for State Enterprises
32	Sofyan A. Djalil	State Minister for Information and Communication
33	Muhammad Yusuf Asy'ari	State Minister for Public Housing
34	Adhyaksa Dault	State Minister for Youth and Sports Affairs
35	Abdul Rachman Saleh	Attorney General
36	Sudi Silalahi[1]	Cabinet Secretary

Note: [1] This name is not mentioned in the "Salinan Keputusan Presiden Republik Indonesia Nomor 187/M Tahun 2004".

Source: Salinan Keputusan Presiden Republik Indonesia Nomor 187/M Tahun 2004.

The members of the cabinet are mostly in their fifties, with four in their forties. Furthermore, the rising standard of education in Indonesia has provided Yudhoyono–Kalla with an opportunity to recruit most members of the cabinet with at least a Masters degree (S-2). Yudhoyono himself received a doctoral degree from the Institute of Agriculture in Bogor on 2 October 2004, not long before he was sworn in as the new president.

Yudhoyono–Kalla attempted to recruit members of the cabinet from many parties, including those who opposed them during the elections. Among his allied parties, they include Yusril Ihza Mahendra and M.S. Kaban of the PBB, Meutia Farida Hatta Swasono of the PKPI, Taufik Effendi and Jero Wacik of the PD, M.Yusuf Asy'ari and Anton Apriyanto of the PKS, Sugiharto and Surya Dharma Ali of the PPP, Bambang Sudibyo and Hatta Rajasa of the PAN, and Saifullah Jusuf and Alwi Shihab of the PKB. From the parties which opposed their candidacy, they include Fahmi Idris and Aburizal Bakrie of Golkar. It should be noted that Golkar was an important member of the National Coalition, which did not support Yudhoyono–Kalla. The internal conflict within Golkar resulted in Fahmi Idris and Aburizal Bakrie taking the side of Yudhoyono–Kalla, rather than joining Akbar Tanjung in the National Coalition. In addition, Adyaksa Dault, a member of the Wiranto–Wahid campaign team and former chairperson of KNPI, was also appointed as a member of the cabinet.

Some of the cabinet members are those who joined the Yudhoyono–Kalla campaign team. Widodo Adi Sutjipto was a senior advisor to Yudhoyono during his campaign; Muhammad Ma'ruf, the chairman of Yudhoyono campaign team and Taufik Effendi, Yudhoyono's advisor in the campaign team. Three ambassadors were called to serve as members of the cabinet. They are Muhammad Maftuh Basyuni, the ambassador to Saudi Arabia as well as a member of NU, Juwono Sudarsono, the ambassador to the United Kingdom, and Freddy Numberi, the ambassador to the Vatican.

All ministers were required to sign a political contract to be loyal, honest, hard-working, giving priority to state and national interests over parties' interests, and to be free from corruption and misconduct. If they were found guilty, they should be prepared to resign from their positions and receive sanctions. The obligation of the signing was to create good governance, free from corruption. Thus, the ministers were expected to be role models for all civil servants and the people, to avoid corruption and other misconducts.

The cabinet was far from perfect. Even President Yudhoyono noted this when he was announcing the cabinet line-up. However, he believed that this was the best he could do. Foreign press criticized the economic team in the cabinet which was led by a politician and a tycoon rather than a professional. It is perhaps still too early to judge whether the cabinet will be able to achieve its objective. It seems that Yudhoyono–Kalla has produced a pro-business and pro-market cabinet with a great willingness to work with international communities. In addition, there is also a sign that the cabinet may apply its pro-business and pro-market orientation to the traditionally "non-economic" sectors such as health and education.

The appointment of some members of the cabinet, for instance Abdurrachman Saleh who is known for his courage and fairness, also indicates the willingness of the government to properly implement the rule of law, in particular in combating corruption. Nevertheless, in a country where corruption is deeply rooted and rampant, the eradication of corruption cannot be achieved in a short time. In fact, the new government faces numerous problems and challenges.

The First Hundred Days of the
Yudhoyono–Kalla Administration

Achievements

Yudhoyono–Kalla's administration has been able to maintain the present economic performance and economic stability in the first hundred days of his administration, while terrorist leaders are still at large. Though in his first hundred days there were no major terrorist attacks, the problem of terrorism was not resolved. His record on combating corruption was also modest; no high-profile offenders had been prosecuted. Nevertheless, President Yudhoyono openly stated that he would continue his efforts to combat corruption. With regard to investment, economists argue that foreign investment in Indonesia has not improved.

The tsunami disaster, which took place on 26 December 2004, was a major crisis for Indonesia. North Sumatra and especially Nanggroe Aceh Darussalam were badly hit. Not only Indonesia but also the whole world has paid special attention to this tragedy. In the few weeks after the tsunami disaster, the Indonesian efforts focused on this. This diverted President Yudhoyono's attention, resulting in his inability to focus on other programmes.

The natural disaster had two impacts for the administration. First, it killed more than 200,000 people, and left a large number of survivors in a traumatized and hopeless situation. The human loss has been tragic, but the economic impact on the Indonesian economy as a whole was very small. Second, it brought in massive foreign aid to Indonesia which might help the Indonesian economy. There was an infrastructure summit in Indonesia after the tsunami tragedy which would give an opportunity for foreign investment to be involved in the reconstruction of Aceh and the affected areas. Besides, this also gave an opportunity to the Yudhoyono government to initiate an offer for the Aceh separatist movement. However, the results for both moves are not yet clear at this juncture.

In the first hundred days of his administration, Yudhoyono had made very modest achievements. Some analysts noted that many things could not be done within a hundred days. Capital investment, for instance, will take at least a year before it starts flowing back. As stated by two observers in the *Jakarta Post*, "For sure it will take 1,000 days, or even more, to rid the country of its terrorists, put more people back to work and bring about a cleaner government."[6]

Rivalry

It should be pointed out that Yudhoyono's party, PD, was a new and small party, which only gained 7.5 per cent of the votes during the April election. His "People's Coalition" has to face a stronger "National Coalition" in parliament. The former obtained only 120 seats while the latter has 267 seats (excluding the PPP). The minority position of Yudhoyono in parliament is certainly a problem, and he needs to gain majority support in order to pass government-sponsored bills. In fact, the first challenge was his act to restore the resigned chief of staff, which was opposed by the parliament. Although there was eventually a compromise, it shows the precarious status of the president.

The election of Agung Laksono from the National Coalition, who had supported Megawati–Hasyim, as the general chairperson of the parliament has made Yudhoyono–Kalla's position more difficult. On the other hand, the success of the People's Coalition, which backed Yudhoyono–Kalla, in placing Hidayat Nur Wahid as the general chairman of the MPR has strengthened the political standing of the Yudhoyono administration. In other words, it may be difficult for the opposition to impeach the president as such an impeachment would have to go through the MPR.

Though Yudhoyono–Kalla has won the presidential elections, the war among the political élites has not ended. The big battle among different interest groups was the formation of the cabinet. Jusuf Kalla was reported to have brought his own men into the cabinet. It had then been a rainbow cabinet, reflecting a lot of compromises to please as many groups as possible, unlike the promise of a limited coalition with more professionals in the cabinet, offered during the campaign. The creation of the "compromise cabinet" may reflect the president's worry of possible "disturbance" (*gangguan*) from the National Coalition, which occupies more than half of the seats in parliament, and from some of his allies.

The 2004 December national congress of Golkar may have reduced the worries of the Yudhoyono administration, as Jusuf Kalla (the vice president) had been elected as the chairman of the Golkar for the 2004–09 term, defeating pro-Megawati Akbar Tanjung. With Kalla as the leader, it is likely that Golkar will cooperate with the government, at least in the foreseeable future.

However, with the growing power in Kalla's hands — he is a businessman, he has the bureaucratic power as the vice president, and he has the political power in the parliament as the general chairman of Golkar — rivalry between Yudhoyono and Kalla may have emerged. The tsunami disaster has highlighted the difference between President Yudhoyono and his deputy Jusuf Kalla.

During the tsunami disaster, the media highlighted various initiatives taken by Jusuf Kalla and the differences between the president and his deputy on their views regarding the role of foreign troops in the affected areas and their length of stay. Some also questioned the legality of Kalla's "vice presidential decision" which was supposed to be the prerogative of the president. Nevertheless, there has not been an open split between the two leaders, and it is likely that they will continue to cooperate as both need each other in the foreseeable future.

On the assumption that the Yudhoyono–Kalla coalition continues, the greater challenge for Yudhoyono–Kalla may not come from the political élites, especially those in parliament, but from the people who have expected too much from him and want to see immediate results.

Continuing Quest for Democracy

The success of Indonesia in strengthening democracy has brought more expectations among the Indonesians. However, the sudden earthquake and tsunami disaster in restive Aceh have required both national and international resources to rehabilitate the affected areas and rebuild the province — and this disaster may have various long-term economic and political implications which still cannot be clearly seen at the time of writing this book.

About four months after he came to power, Yudhoyono, in his lecture entitled "Indonesia: The Challenge of Change" delivered on 16 February 2005 in Singapore, stated:

> My mission as the sixth president of Indonesia is to advance as far as possible Indonesia's democracy and *reformasi*. What I promised the Indonesian voters were quite simple: To do my best to make Indonesia more democratic, more peaceful, more just, more prosperous. And I intend to keep that promise.

Indeed, the world is anxiously watching the emerging democracy in Indonesia, a country with the fourth largest population and the largest number of Muslims in the world. The democratic elections may have some implications in the region and beyond. However, whether or not this model is applicable to other countries remains to be seen. Indonesia has already had peaceful democratic elections and shown that a Muslim majority state does not have to be a Muslim or Islamic state as defined in political science. The Indonesian experience may have illustrated the success of democracy in a country with Muslims as the majority. However, this peaceful transformation from authoritarianism to democracy is not without problems. Nevertheless, it appears that democracy is working, and hopefully it will gradually become Indonesia's political culture.

Notes

1. Khamami Zada, "Partai Islam dan Pemilu 2004", *Kompas*, 19 December 2004. The PAN and PKB are not included here because they are not Islamic parties, though perceived as Islamic parties with PAN often associated with modernist Islam and the PKB with traditionalist Islam.
2. Historiografi SBY, *Kompas,* 24 June 2004.
3. "Menjadi Tentara adalah Cita-Cita SBY Kecil", *Kompas*, 24 June 2004.

4. "Wibowo, Sarwo Edhie" in *Apa & Siapa: Sejumlah Orang Indonesia 1985–1986*. Jakarta: Grafiti Pers, 1986, pp. 1179–80.
5. Sukardi Rinakit, *The Indonesian Military after the New Order*. Denmark & Singapore: NIAS and ISEAS, 2005, ch. 3.
6. James Van Zorge and Dennis Heffernan, "The Myth of the First 100 Days and Susilo's Real Challenges", *Jakarta Post*, 1 October 2004.

APPENDIX 1.1

Members of House of Representatives from GOLKAR, 2004–09

No.	Province	Name	No.	Province	Name
1	Nanggroe Aceh Darussalam	Hj. Marliah Amin	21	South Sumatra	Ir. A. Hafiz Zawawi, MSc
2		Drs. T. Muhammad Nurlif	22	Bengkulu	Drs. H. Sulaeman Effendi
3	North Sumatra	Drs. H. N. Serta Ginting	23	Lampung	Ir. Agusman Effendi
4		Antarini Malik	24		Drs. H. Djoko Purwongemboro
5		Rambe Kamarul Zaman, MSc	25		Drs. H. Riswan Tony DK
6		Drs. M. Syarfi Hutauruk	26		M. Azis Syamsuddin
7		Drs. Mahadi Sinambela, MSi	27	Bangka Belitung	Ir. H. Azhar Romli, MSi
8		Dr. H. Bomer Pasaribu, SH, SE, MS	28	Riau Archipelago	Dr. H. Harry Azhar Azis, MA
9	West Sumatra	H. Aulia Aman Rachman, SH, MSi	29	Jakarta	H.R. Agung Laksono
10		Dr. H.M. Azwir Dainy Tara, MBA	30		Drs. H. Fahmi Idris
11		Drs. H. Darul Siska	31	West Java	Dr. Happy Bone Zulkarnain, MS
12		H. Djusril Djusan, SH	32		Drs. H.M. Paskah Suzetta, MBA
13	Riau	H. Saleh Djasit, SH	33		Ferry Mursyidan Baldan
14		H. Azwar Chesputra, SE	34		Dr. Ir. H. Lili Asdjudiredja, SE
15		Musfihin Dahlan	35		Drg. H. Tonny Aprilani, MSc
16	Jambi	Drs. Antony Zedra Abidin	36		Drs. H. Deding Ishak, SH, MM
17		Drs. Ismail Tajuddin	37		Dewi Asmara, SH
18	South Sumatra	Drs. Ridwan Mukti, MBA	38		Adiwarsita Adinegoro
19		Drs. Kahar Muzakir	39		Drs. Mohammad Hatta, MBA
20		H. Marzuki Achmad, SH	40		Ir. H. Awal Kusumah, MS

continued on next page

APPENDIX 1.1 – cont'd

No.	Province	Name	No.	Province	Name
41	West Java	Ir. H. Airlangga Hartarto, MMT, MBA	61	Central Java	Bobby Satrio Hardiwibowo Suhardiman
42		Moh. S. Hidayat	62		Drs. H. Priyo Budi Santoso
43		Drs. H. Zulkarnaen Djabar, MA	63		Drs. Slamet Effendy Yusuf, MSi
44		Drs. Ade Komarudin	64		H. Dito Ganinduto, MBA
45		Drs. H. Wasma Prayitno	65		Drs. A.H. Mujib Rohmat
46		Drs. Engartiasto Lukita	66		Drs. H. Mohammad Ichwan Syam
47		H. Yuddy Chrisnandi, ME	67	Yogyakarta	GBPH H. Joyokusumo
48		Budi Harsono	68	East Java	Joko Subroto
49		Drs. H. Eldie Suwandie	69		Dra. Hj. Faridah Effendy
50		Drs. Agun Gunandjar Sudarsa	70		H. Hardisoesilo
51		Dra. Hj. Maryamah Nugraha Besoes	71		Ir. H. Herman Widyananda, SE, MSi
52		H. Asep Ruchimat Sudjana	72		Hj. Tyas Indyah Iskandar, SH, MKn
53		H. Abdul Nurhaman, SIP, SSos, MSi	73		Drs. HM. Irsyad Sudiro, MSi
54		Ferdiansyah, SE, MM	74		M. Yahya Zaini, SH
55	Central Java	Drs. K.H. Ahmad Darodji	75		Dr. HM Markum Singodimejo
56		Nusron Wahid	76		Hayani Isman
57		Dra. Sri Harini	77		Hj. Soedarmani Wiryatmo, SH, MHum
58		Bambang Sadono, SH, MH	78		Aisyah Hamid Baidlowi
59		Drs. Hajriyanto Y. Thohari, MA	79		Drs. E.C.H. Soekotjo Said
60		Ir. H. Soeharsoyo	80		Drs. Imam Supardi

81	Banten	Dr. H.M. Irsjad Djuwaeli
82		Mamat Rahayu Abdulah
83		Drs. Muhammad Aly Yahya
84		H. Ebby Djauharie
85		Budiarsa Sastrawinata
86	Bali	Gde Sumarjaya Linggih, SE
87		Tisnawati Karna, SH
88	West Nusa Tenggara	Marzuki Darusman, SH
89		H. Mesir Suryadi, SH
90		Adi Putra Darmawan Tahir
91	East Nusa Tenggara	Josef A. Nae Soi
92		Melchias Markus Mekeng
93		Drs. Setya Novanto
94		Dr. Charles J. Mesang
95		Victor Bungtilu Laiskodat, SH.
96	West Kalimantan	M. Akil Mokhtar, SH, MH
97		H. Gusti Syamsumin
98		Asiah Salenka, BA
99	Central Kalimantan	Dra. Chairunnisa, MA
100		Mochtaruddin
101	South Kalimantan	H. Gusti Iskandar Sukma Alamsyah, SE
102		H. Hasanuddin Murad, SH
103	East Kalimantan	H.A. Afifuddin Thalib, SH
104		H. Muhayan Hasan
105	North Sulawesi	Drs. Theo L. Sambuaga
106		Drs. H. Djelantik Mokodompit
107	Central Sulawesi	M. Sofhian Mile, SH
108		Muhidin M. Said, SE, MBA
109	Southeast Sulawesi	Prof. Drs. H. Rustam E. Tamburaka, MA
110		Dra. Hj. Mustika Rahim
111	South Sulawesi	Andi Mattalatta, SH, MH
112		Prof. Dr. H. Anwar Arifin
113		H. Hamka Yandhu Y. R, SE
114		Idrus Marham
115		Ny. Nurhayati Yasin Limpo
116		H. Syamsul Bachri, M.Sc
117		Dr. Marwah Daud Ibrahim, MA
118		H.M. Malkan Amin
119		Drs. Fachri Andi Leluasa
120		Dr. Hj. Mariani Akib Baramuli, MM
121	Gorontalo	Zainuddin Amali, SE
122		Ny. Dra. Truliyanti S. Habibie, MPsi
123	Maluku	Ir. Hamzah Sangadji
124	North Maluku	Dr. H. Abdul Gafur
125	West Irian Jaya	Robert Joppy Kardinal
126	Papua	Simon Patrice Morin
127		Yorris T. H. Raweyai
128		Drs. Freddy Latumahina

Note: Drs. and Dra. are titles for those who completed the undergraduate degree and refer to the gender of an individual. Drs. is for a man and Dra. for a woman. SH, SE, Ir, SSos, SAg are also titles for those who completed undergraduate studies on a particular subject/course. SH (Sarjana Hukum) is for law studies, SE (Sarjana Ekonomi) for economics, Ir (Insinyur) for engineering studies, SSos (Sarjana Social) for Social Studies and SAg (sarjana Agama) for Islamic studies) MA, MM, MBA, MH, MS, MSi and MSc are title for those who completed the master's degree.

Source: Compiled from http://www.kpu.go.id

APPENDIX 1.2
Members of House of Representatives from the PDI-P, 2004–09

No.	Province	Name	No.	Province	Name
1	North Sumatra	H. Irmadi Lubis	29	West Java	Dr. Goenawan Slamet, SpB
2		Dr. Y. H. Laoly, SH. MSc	30		Drs. Shidarito Danusubroto, SH
3		Trimedya Panjaitan, SH	31		Mayjen Pol. Purn. Suryana
4		Idham, SH, MKN	32		Yosep Umar Hadi
5		Taufan Tampubolon, SE	33		Djoemad Cipto Wardoyo
6	Riau	H. Fachruddin S	34		Marliarar Sirait, SIP
7	Jambi	Dra. Elviana, MSi	35		Endang Karman
8	Bengkulu	Hj. Elva Hartarti M.SIP	36		Drs. Eka Santosa
9	South Sumatra	Ir. Nazarudin Kiemas	37		E.A. Darojat
10		H. Dudhie Makmun Murod, MBA	38	Central Java	Ir. Daniel Budi Setiawan, MM
11	Lampung	Suparlan, SH	39		Dra. Nurhayati
12		Ir. Isma Yatun	40		Deddy Sutomo
13		Pataniari Siahaan	41		Agung Sasongko
14		Dr. Sukowaluyo M	42		Tjahjo Kumolo
15	Bangka Belitung	Ir. Rudianto Tjen	43		Dr. A. Sonny Keraf
16	Riau Archipelago	Jaka Aryadipa Singgih	44		Dra. Hj. Siti Soepami
17		H. Soekardjo Hardjosoewirdjo, SH	45		Drs. H. Sumaryoto
18	Jakarta	Drs. Effendi M.S. Simbolon	46		Ir. Bambang Wuryanto, MBA
19		H. Roy BB Janis, SH	47		Tjandra Widjaja
20	West Java	Mangara M. Siahaan	48		Gunawan Wirosaroyo
21		H. Moh. Taufiq Kiemas	49		Nusyirwan Soejono
22		Marissa Haque	50		Y. Aria Bima Trihastoto
23		H. Amris Fuad Hasan, MA	51		Drs. H. Marjono
24		Dr. Ribka Tjiptaning	52		Prof. Dr. Sudigdo A
25		Dra. Hj. Noviantika Nasution	53		Drh. H. Soeratal HW
26		Philip S. Widjaja	54		Drs. Jakob Tobing, MPA
27		Zainal Arifin	55		Ir. Hendarso Hadi Pramono, MBA
28		Panda Nababan	56		Nadrah Izahari, SH

No.	Region	Name	No.	Region	Name
57	Central Java	A. Condro Prayitno	84	Banten	Ir. Arifin Panigoro
58		H.R. Pupung Suharis, SH	85	Banten	Hj. Tumbu Saraswati, SH
59		Chepy Triprakoso Wartono, SE	86		Drs. K. Dharmono K. Lawi
60		Widodo Bujo Wiryono	87		H. Wowo Ibrahim
61		Ramson Siagian	88	Bali	I Gusti Ngurah Sara
62	Yogyakarta	A.H. Soetardjo S, BA	89		I Gusti Agung Ray Wirajaya, SE, MM
63		Dra. Edi Mihati, MSi	90		Drs. I Made Urip
64	East Java	Ir. H. Sutjipto	91		Dr. Ir. Wayan Koster, MM
65		L. Soepomo SW, SH	92		Ni Gusti Ayu Eka Sukma Dewi
66		Murdaya Poo	93	West Nusa Tenggara	H. Mudahir
67		Drs. Soewarno	94	East Nusa Tenggara	Drs. Cyprianus Aoer
68		Nur Suhud	95		Theo Syafei
69		Imam Suroso	96	East Nusa Tenggara	Herman Hery
70		Drs. Tukidjo	97	West Kalimantan	Maxmoein, MA, MBA
71		Ir. H. Pramono Anung W, MM	98		Drs. Agustinus Clarus
72		Dr. Gayus Lumbuun, SH	99	Central Kalimantan	Agustin Teras Narang, SH
73		M. Guruh Soekarnoputra	100	East Kalimantan	Ir. Izedrik Emir Moeis, MSc
74		Drs. W. Eko Waluyo	101	South Kalimantan	Royani Haminullah
75		Ir. Theodorus J.K	102	North Sulawesi	Olly Dondokambey, SE
76		Ir. H. Heri Achmadi	103	Central Sulawesi	Ir. H. Rendy Lamadjito
77		Ir. Hasto Kristiyanto, MM	104	South Sulawesi	H. Anwar Fatta
78		Suwignyo	105		Jacobus Mayong Padang
79		Ir. Mindo Sianipar	106	Southeast Sulawesi	Drs. H. A. Razak Porosi
80	East Java	Dr. Drs. H. Moch. Hasib Wahab	107	Maluku	Alexander Litaay
81		Permadi, SH	108	West Irian Jaya	Raja K. Sembiring
82		Ida Bagus N, SH	109	Papua	Drs. Ben Vincent Djeharu, MM
83		H.M. Said Abdullah			

APPENDIX 1.3
Members of House of Representatives from PPP, 2004–09

No.	Province	Name	No.	Province	Name
1	Nanggroe Aceh Darussalam	Tgk Muhammad Yus	30	Central Java	Drs. H. Arief Mudatsir Mandan, MSi
2		Dr. H. Muchtar Aziz, MA	31		H. M. Faqih Chaeroni
3	North Sumatra	Drs. Hasrul Azwar, MA	32		H. Ahmad Thoyfoer, Mc
4		H. Musa Ichwanshah, SH MH	33		Drs. H Lukman Hakim Saifuddin
5		Maiyasyak Johan	34		H. Daromi Irdjas, SH MSi
6	West Sumatra	Efiyardi Asda	35		Drs. H Zainut Tauhid Sa'adi
7		H. Yudo Paripurno, SH	36		H. Djuhad Mahja, SH CN
8	Riau	H. Syahrial Agamas	37		Drs. H. Tosari Widjaya
9	Jambi	H. Achmad Farial	38		Usamah Muhammad Al Hadar
10	Bengkulu	H. M. Al Amin Nur Nasution, SE	39		H.M. Syumli Syadli, SH
11	South Sumatra	Drs. H. Djabaruddin Ahmad	40		Mahsusoh Ujiati
12		H. Romzi Nihan, S. IP	41		Drs. H.A. Hafidz Ma'Soem
13	Lampung	Hj. Sundari Fitriyana, SAg	42		Hj Machfudhoh Aly Ubaid
14	Jakarta	Drs. H Suryadharma Ali, MSi	43		H. Sulaeman Fadeli
15		H. A Chudlory Syafei Hadzami, SSos	44		K.H. Ismail Muzakki
16	West Java	H. Burhanudin Somawinata	45	Banten	Drs. H Sa'adun Syibromalisi
17		Drs. H. Ahmad Kurdi Moekri	46		H. Idiel Suryadi, BSc
18		H. Chairul Anwar Lubis	47	West Nusa Tenggara	K.H. Muhammad Anwar, MA
19		Drs. H. Lukman Hakiem	48	West Kalimantan	H. Uray Faisal Hamid, SH
20		H. Endang Kosasih, MA SE	49	East Kalimantan	H.M. Hifni Sarkawie
21		H. Sofyan Usman	50	Central Kalimantan	H. Rusnain Yahya
22		Ir. A Rahman Syagaff	51	South Kalimantan	H. Syafriansyah, BA
23		Drs. HB Tamam Achda	52		H. Husairi Abdi, Lc
24		K.H. Ma'Mur Noor	53	North Sulawesi	Sukardi Harun
25		Drs. H Anwar Sanusi, SH MH	54	Central Sulawesi	H. Yusuf Rizal Tjokroaminoto
26		Drs. HA Chozin Chumaidy	55	South Sulawesi	H. Andi M Ghalib, SH MH
27		Drs. H Endin A.J. Soefihara, MMA	56		H.M. Yunus Yosfiah
28		K.H. Amin Bunyamin, Lc	57	Southeast Sulawesi	H. Habil Marati, SE
29	Central Java	Drs. Akhmad Muqowam	58	Gorontalo	H. Suharso Monoarfa

APPENDIX 1.4
Members of House of Representatives from PD, 2004–09

No.	Province	Name	No.	Province	Name
1	Nanggroe Aceh Darussalam	Prof. Dr. Rusli Ramli, MS	29	Yogyakarta	Ir Budi Prihandoko, MTP
2		Mirwan Amir	30	Central Java	Vera Febyanthi, BBA
3	North Sumatra	Ir. H. Moh. Yusuf Pardamean, Nst	31		Shidki Wahab
4		Drs. Saidi Butar Butar	32		MayJen(Purn) Ignatius Mulyono
5		Maruahal Silalahi	33		FX Soekarno, SH
6	West Sumatra	H. Dasrul Djabar	34		H. Soekartono Hadi Warsito
7	Jambi	Drs. H. Syofyan	35		Angelina Sondakh, SE
8	Riau	Prof. Ph.D. Mirrian Sjofyan Arief, MEc	36		Burhanuddin Bur Maras
9	South Sumatra	Dr H Hakim Sorimuda Pohan, SPog	37		Suryo Superno
10		Sarjan Tahir, SE. MM	38	East Java	Marcus Silanno, SIP
11	Lampung	Drs. H. Sutan Bhatoegana, MM	39		Ir. Chandra Pratomo Samiadji Massaid
12		Dr. Ir. Atte Sugandi, MM	40		H. Azzam Azman Natawijana
13	Banten	H. Zaenuddin	41		H. Sunarto Muntako
14		Dr. Ir. Denny Sultani Hasan	42		Hasanuddin Said, AK
15		Prof. Dr. Irzan Tanjung	43		Dr. H Achmad Fauzi, SH MM
16	Jakarta	Chufran Hamal, SH	44		Soetadji, SE. SIP, MM
17		H. Tri Yulianto, SH	45		Drs. H Guntur Sasono, MSi
18		Ir. H Husein Abdul Aziz, MT	46		Drs. Balkan Kaplale
19		Indria Octavia Muaja	47	Bali	I Wayan Gunastra
20	West Java	H. Daday Hudaya	48	West Nusa Tenggara	Drs. I Wayan Sugiana, MM
21		Ir. H. Roestanto Wahidi Dirdjojuwono, MM	49	East Nusa Tenggara	Anita Yacob A Gah
22		Syarifuddin Hasan, SE. MM, MBA	50	West Kalimantan	Albert Yaputra
23		Max Sopacua, SE. MSc	51	South Kalimantan	Drs. Taufiq Effendi, MBA
24		Dr. H Tata Zainal Mutaqin, MM	52	Central Kalimantan	Drs. Barnstein Samuel Tundan
25		Boy MW Saul	53	East Kalimantan	Dr. (HC) Hj Adji Farida Padmo
26		Ir. Agus Hermanto, MM	54	North Sulawesi	Evert Erenst Mangindaan, SE SIP
27		Drs. Nurul Qomar	55	South Sulawesi	Junus Efendi Habibie
28		H. Aziddin, SE			

APPENDIX 1.5
Members of House of Representatives from PAN, 2004–09

No.	Province	Name	No.	Province	Name
1	Nanggroe Aceh Darussalam	H. Imam Syuja, SE	28	Central Java	Alvin Lie Ling Piao
2		Dr. Ahmad Farhan Hamid, MS	29		Tuti Indarsih Loekman Soetrisno
3	North Sumatra	Mulfachri Harahap, SH	30		Dr. Marwoto Mitrohardjono, SE, MM
4		Ir. Akmaldin Noor, MBA	31		Ir. Tjatur Sapto Edy. MT
5		Nasril Bahar, SE	32		Ir. Taufik Kurniawan, MM
6	West Sumatra	Patrialis Akbar, SH	33		Dr. Fuad Bawazier, MA
7		Ir. Ichwan Ishak, MSi	34		Drs. H. Munawar Sholeh
8	Riau	Hj. Azlaini Agus, SH, MM	35		Drs. Abdul Hakam Naja
9	Jambi	Drs. H. Rizal Djalil, MM	36	Yogyakarta	H. Totok Daryanto, SE
10	South Sumatra	M. Joko Santoso, SSos	37		Dra. Latifah Iskandar
11		Ir. Putra Jaya Husin	38	East Java	Drs. Djoko Susilo, MA
12	Bengkulu	H. Hermansyah Nazirun, SH	39		Prof. Dr. Didiek J. Rachbini
13	Lampung	Zulkifli SE, MM	40		Achmad Affandi
14		Hj. Nidalia Djohansyah Makki	41		Drs. Mardiana Indraswati
15	Riau Archipelago	Asmar Abnur, SE	42		Ir. Muhammad Najib, MSc
16	Jakarta	Dr. Ir. Drajat Hari Wibowo, MEC	43		Djoko Edhi Soetjipto Abdurahman
17		Ir. Afni Achmad	44	West Nusa Tenggara	Nazamuddin, SE
18	West Java	Ir. M. Hatta Rajasa	45	West Kalimantan	H. Ishaq Saleh
19		Drs. Dedy Djamaluddin M, Msi	46	Central Kalimantan	Drs. Nurul Falah Eddy Pariang
20		Ir. Sayuti Asyatry	47	East Kalimantan	Mohammad Yasin Kara, SE
21		H. Sabri Saiman	48	South Kalimantan	Jumanhuri, S.Pd
22		Drs. H.A.M. Fatwa	49	South Sulawesi	Ir. Abdul Hadi Jamal
23		H. Ade Firdaus, SE	50		Hj. Andi Yuliani Paris
24		Yusuf Macan Effendy	51	Southeast Sulawesi	Arbab Papoeka, SH
25		Ir. Tristanti Mitayani, MT	52	Central Sulawesi	Nurhadi M Musawir, SH, MM, MBA
26	Banten	Ir. Tubagus Rizon Sofhani	53	Papua	Sudjud Siradjuddin, SH, MH
27		Abdillah Toha			

APPENDIX 1.6
Members of House of Representatives from PKB, 2004–09

No.	Province	Name	No.	Province	Name
1	Riau	HM. Khaidir M. Wafa	27	East Java	H.M. Irfan Zidhy, MA
2	South Sumatra	Dr. H. Ishartanto, SE, MMA	28		Drs. Amin Said Husni
3	Lampung	Ahmad Syafrin Romas	29		Ahmad Anas Yahya
4	West Java	Dr. Muhammad A.S. Hikam	30		Drs. H. Yusuf Muhammad, LML
5		A. Helmi Faishal Zaini	31		Choirul Saleh Rasyid, SE
6		Drs. H. Mohammad Dahlan Chudori	32		H. Ali Mudhori SAg MAg
7	Central Java	H.Z. Arifin Junaidi	33		Dra. Hj. Anisah Mahfudz
8		Drs. Mufid A Busyairi MPD	34		Drs. H. Saifullah Ma'shum
9		Dra. Badriyah Fayumi Lc	35		Drs. Ali Masykur Musa, MSi
10		Marwan, SH, SE	36		H. Imam Anshori Saleh, SH
11		Drs. Mufid Rahmat	37		H. Imam Nahrawi, SAg
12		Ir. H. Erman Suparno, MBA, Msi	38		Drs. H.M. Subki Risya
13		H. Idham Cholied, SSos	39		Muhyidin Arubusman
14		R. Saleh Abdul Malik	40		M. Hasyim Karim, SH
15		Prof. Drs. H. Cecep Syarifuddin	41		Dra. Hj. Ida Fauziah
16		K.H. Hanief Ismail, LC	42		A. Effendy Choirie, MAg, MH
17		Bachruddin Nasori, SSi, MM	43		Hj. Anna Mu'awanah, SE
18		Dr. H. Alwi Abdurrahman Shihab	44		Masduki Baidlowi
19		Drs. H. Bisri Romli, MM	45		H. Taufikurrahman Saleh, SH, MSi
20	Yogyakarta	Hj. Zunnatul Mafruchah, SH	46		Prof. Dr. Moh Mahfud MD
21	East Java	Drs. H.A. Muhaimin Iskandar, MSi	47		H. Imam Buchori Cholil
22		Khofifah Indar Parawansa	48		Ilyas Siraj, SH, MAg
23		H. Ario Wijanarko, SH	49	Banten	Drs. H.M. Arsa Suthisna, MM
24		Syaifullah Yusuf	50		Dr. Ir. H.M. Yusuf Faishal, MSc
25		Nursyahbani Kacasungkana, SH	51	South Kalimantan	H.L. Misbah Hidayat
26	East Java	K.H. Ahmad Rawi	52	Papua	Tony Wardoyo

APPENDIX 1.7
Members of House of Representatives from PKS, 2004–09

No.	Province	Name	No.	Province	Name
1	Nanggroe Aceh Darussalam	M. Nasir Jamil, SAg	24	West Java	K.H. Yusuf Supendi, Lc
2		Andi Salahudin, SE	25		Hj. Yoyoh Yusroh
3	North Sumatra	Drs. Muhammad Idris Luthfi, MSc	26		Dh. Al Yusni
4	West Sumatra	Ansory Siregar	27		H.A. Najiyullih, Lc
5		Irwan Prayitno	28		R. Bagus Suryama Majana S Psi
6		Refrizal	29		Drs. Mahfudz Siddiq, MSi
7	Riau	Drs. Chairul Anwar, Apt	30		Wahyudin Munawir
8	Jambi	Ir. Ami Taher	31		H. Umung Anwar Sanusi, Lc
9	South Sumatra	Mustafa Kamal, SS	32		H. Hilman Rosyad Syihab
10	Lampung	Drs. Al Muzzammil Yusuf	33	Yogyakarta	Agus Purnomo, SIP
11		K.H. Ir. Abdul Hakim, MM	34	Central Java	Zuber Safawi, SH
12	Banten	Abdi Sumaithi	35		Mutammimul Ula, SH
13		Dr. Zulkieflimansyah, S, MSc	36		Ir. H. Suswono
14		H. Jazuli Juwaini, Lc	37	East Java	Suripto, SH
15	Jakarta	Muhammad Anis Matta, Tks	38		Luthfi Hasan Ishaaq
16		Nursanita Nasution, SE, ME	39	West Nusa Tenggara	Fahri Hamzah, SE
17		Rama Pratama, SE, Ak	40	South Kalimantan	Aboe Bakar
18		Dr. M. Hidayat Nur Wahid, MA	41	East Kalimantan	H. Ahmad Chudori
19		Dra. Hj. Aan Rohana, MAg	42	South Sulawesi	Tamsil Linrung
20	West Java	H. Rahmat Abdullah	43		H.M. Seniman Latif, SE
21		Ma'mur Hasanuddin	44	North Maluku	H. Abdul Gani Kasuba
22		Drs. H. Djalaluddin Asysyafibi	45	Maluku	H. Abdul Aziz Arbi
23		Ir. H. Untung Wahono, MSi			

APPENDIX 1.8
Members of House of Representatives from Other Parties*, 2004–09

No.	Province	Name
	PBR	
1	Nanggroe Aceh Darussalam	Anhar, SE
2		Zainal Abidin Hussein, SE
3	North Sumatra	H. Zaenal Ma'arif, SH, MAg
4		H. Nasaruddin Pasaribu
5		Hj. Zul Hizwar SPsi
6	West Sumatra	H. Is Anwar
7	South Sumatra	Bursah Zarnubi, SE
8	Riau	H. Bulyan Royan
9	Banten	H. Ade Daud Iswandi
10	West Nusa Tenggara	L. Gede Syamsul Mujahidin, SE
11	West Kalimantan	H. Rusman H.M. Ali, SH
12	South Kalimantan	H. Yusuf Fanie Andin Kasim, SH
13	South Sulawesi	Mayjend. Purn. Andi Djalal Bachtiar
14		Dr. Diah Defawati
	PDS	
1	North Sumatra	Drs. Hasurungan Simamora
2		Rufinus Sianturi, SH, MH
3		St. Drs. Jansen Hutasoit, SE, MM Kol Pol
4	Jakarta	Tiurlan Basaria Hutagaol
5		Constant M. Ponggawa, SH
6	West Java	Carol D. Yani Kadang, SE MM
7	East Nusa Tenggara	Ruth Nina M. Kedang, SE
8	West Kalimantan	Walman Siahaan, SE, MM
9	North Sulawesi	Jeffrey Johanes Massie
10	Central Sulawesi	Retna Rosmanita Situmorang, MBA
11	Maluku	John M. Toisuta
12	West Irian Jaya	Pastor Saut M. Hasibuan
13	Papua	Ir. Apri Hananto Sukandar, MDiv

No.	Province	Name
	PBB	
1	Nanggroe Aceh Darussalam	Muhammad Fauzi, SE
2	West Sumatra	H. Nur Syamsi Nurlan, SH
3		Ir. Nizar Dahlan, MSi
4	Riau	Muhammad Tonas, SE
5	Bangka Belitung	Dr. Yusron Ihza, LLM
6	South Sumatra	Drs. H. Moh. Darus Agap
7	Banten	Hilman Indra, SE, MBA
8	West Java	Ms. Kaban, SE. MSi
9	West Nusa Tenggara	Kh Muhammad Zainul Majdi, MA
10	South Kalimantan	Jamaluddin Karim, SH
11	South Sulawesi	Drs. Ali Mochtar Ngabalin, MSi
	PPDK	
1	South Sulawesi	Prof. DR. m. Ryaas Rasyid, MA
2		Rapiuddin Hamarung
3	North Maluku	Drs. H. Mudafar Syah
4	Papua	Inya Bay, SE, MM
	PP	
1	North Sumatra	Idealisman Dachi
2	East Nusa Tenggara	Anton A. Mashur, SE
3	Papua	Etha Bulo
	PKPB	
1	Bali	Drs. Made Suhendra
2	Lampung	Dion Hardi, BA
	PNIM	
1	Papua	H. Ardy Muhammad, MBA
	PKPI	
1	East Nusa Tenggara	Harman Benediktus Kabur
	PPDI	
1	East Nusa Tenggara	Joseph Williem Lea Wea

Note: * = Other Parties include PBR, PDS, PBB, PPDK, PP, PKPB, PNIM, PKPI and PPDI. PP = Pioneer Party

APPENDIX 2
Members of the Regional Representatives Council (DPD), 2004–09

Name/Province	Name/Province	Name/Province	Name/Province
Nanggroe Aceh Darussalam	**Jambi**	**Bangka Belitung**	**Central Java**
Drs. H.A. Malik Raden, MM	Nuzran Joher, SAg	H. Rosman Djohan	Dra. Hj. Nafisah Sahal
H. Helmi Mahera Al Mujahid	Dra. Hj. Nyimas Ena, MM	Drs. Rusli Rachman, MSi	Ir. H. Budi Santoso
Adnan NS, SSos	Muhammad Nasir	Fajar Fairi Husni, SH	Drs. H. Sudharto, MA.
Dra. Hj. Mediati Hafni Hanum	Drs. H. Hasan	Hj. Djamila Somad, BSc	KH. Ahmad Chalwani
North Sumatra	**South Sumatra**	**Riau Archipelago**	**Yogyakarta**
Drs. H. Abd. Halim Harahap	Hj. Asmawati, SE MM	Aida Ismet	GKR. Hemas
Ir. Nurdin Tampubolon	Drs. H.M. Kafrawi Rahim	Ir. H. Idris Zaini	Drs. H. Ali Warsito
Raja Inal Siregar	Drs. M. Jum Perkasa	Benny Horas Panjaitan	Drs. H. Abdul Hafidh Asrom, MM
Drs. H. Yopie Sangkot Batubara	Ir. Ruslan Wijaya, SE MSc	Hendry Frankim	H. Subardi
West Sumatra	**Bengkulu**	**Jakarta**	**East Jawa**
H. Irman Gusman, SE, MBA	DIPL. ING. Bambang Soeroso	Hj. BRA. Mooryati Soedibyo, SS, MHum	H. Mahmud Ali Zain
Drs. H. Zairin Kasim	H. Mahyudin Shobri, SE	Ir. Sarwono Kusumaatmadja	K.H. A. Mujib Imron, SH
Afdal, SSi	Muspani, SH	H. Biem Triani Benyamin. S	KH. M. Nuruddin A. Rahman, SH
Dr. Muchtar Naim	Dra. Eni Khaerani, MSi	Ir. H. Marwan Batubara, MSc	Drs. H. Mardjito GA
Riau	**Lampung**	**West Java**	**Banten**
Drs. H. Soemardi Thaher	H. Kasmir Tri Putra, SPD, MM	Prof. Dr. Ir. H. Ginandjar Kartasasmita	K.H. Thoyib Amir
Dinawaty, SAg	Hj. Hariyanti Safrin, SH	PRA Arief Natadiningrat, SE	Dra. HJ. Ratu Cicih Kurniasih
Intsiawati Ayus, SH	Sujadi	Prof. Dr. H. Mohamad Surya	H. Apud Mahpud
Dra. Hj. Maimanah Umar	A. Ben Bella	K.H. Sofyan Yahya, MA.	H. Sagap Usman

Bali
I Wayan Sudirta, SH
Nyoman Rudana
Drs. Ida Bagus Gede Agastia
Dra. Ida Ayu Agung Mas

West Nusa Tenggara
Drs. H. Harun Al Rasyid, MSi
Drs. H. Syahdan Ilyas
Drs. H. Lalu Yusuf
H.L. Abdul Muhyi Abidin, SAg

East Nusa Tenggara
Frans X Assan
Drs. Yonathan Nubatonis
Joseph Bona Manggo
Wilhelmus Wua Openg

West Kalimantan
Dr. Piet Herman Abik. MApp, SC
Maria Goreti, SSos, MSi
Sri Kadarwati
H. Aspar, SE

Central Kalimantan
Dr. KH. Haderani H.N
Prof. KMA. M. Usop, MA
H. Abi Kusno Nachran
Permanasari

South Kalimantan
IR. H.M. Said
Drs. H. Muhammad Sofwat Hadi, SH
H.A. Makkie, BA
Drs. H.M. Ramli

East Kalimantan
Drs. Nursyamsa Hadis
Luther Kombong
Ir. Hj. Eka Komariah Kuncoro, MA CED
Ir. HJ. Nur Andriyani

North Sulawesi
Ir. Marhany V.P. PUA
Aryanti Baramuli Putri
Edwin Kawilarang
Dra. Sientje Sondakh ? Mandey

Central Sulawesi
Hj. Nurmawati D. Bantilan, SE
Drs. Roger Tobigo
M. Ichsan Loulembah
Drs. H. Faisal Mahmud

South Sulawesi
H.M. Aksa Mahmud
Ir. H. Abdul Azis Qahar Mudzakkar
Ishak Pamumbu Lambe
Benyamin Bura

Southeast Sulawesi
LA Ode Ida
Drs. K.H. Marwan Aidid
Ir. H.M. Yunus Sjamsoeddin
Drs. H. Yokoyama Sinapoy

Gorontalo
Drs. A.D. Khaly
Prof. Dr. Hl. Nani Tuloli
Hl. Amir Adam
Roeland Niode

Maluku
Ny. Mirati Dewaningsih, ST
Abraham Dominggus Tuapattinaya, BA
Midin B. Lamany, SH
Drs. Hi. H.A. Rahayaan

North Maluku
Anthony Charles Sunarjo
Drs. Juanda Bakar
Ny. Nita Budhi Susanti
Hl. Djafarsyah

West Irian Jaya
Salome Christin Saway, SH
Ishak Mandacan
Dr. Ir. Abdul M. Kilian, MS
Drs. H. Wahidin Ismail

Papua
Marcus Louis Zonggonao, BA
Tonny Tesar
Ferdinanda Ibo Yatifay
Pdt. Drs. Max Demetouw

Note: The seat for K.H. Ahmad Chalwani, Central Java, was previously given to Drs. H. Dahlan Rais, MHum. Based on the constitutional court, Dahlan Rais gained 880.774 votes, the fifth rank, which was 274 votes less than Achmad Chalwani (881,050 votes). "Adik Kandung Amien Rais Akhirnya Gagal Jadi Anggota DPD" 1 June 2004. <http://hukumonline.com/detail.asp?id=10422&cl=Berita>. The decision is stated at the flea no 014/PHPU.A-II/2004 <http://www.ifes.org/reg_activities/docs/Constitutional_Court_Decision_for_DPD_General_Election_Results_Cases_from_Candidates.pdf>.

Source: Compiled from <http://www.kpu.go.id>.

APPENDIX 3.1
The Number of Votes of the 2004 Parliamentary Election Results for DPR-RI by Province

No.	Party	N. Aceh Darussalam	North Sumatra	West Sumatra	Riau	Jambi	South Sumatra	Bengkulu	Lampung
1	PNI	12,566	65,555	9,630	18,115	17,152	52,223	11,353	64,283
2	PBSD	13,537	111,366	12,345	29,972	11,623	23,624	10,620	25,443
3	PBB	111,799	134,461	116,594	83,283	42,632	137,995	29,841	69,197
4	MERDEKA	34,085	52,369	30,270	17,833	14,544	39,964	7,294	17,551
5	PPP	291,410	397,811	234,806	167,858	74,388	218,019	62,270	171,228
6	PPDK	48,850	71,541	18,572	55,897	16,532	49,172	10,272	70,769
7	PPIB	20,337	118,847	13,674	28,829	9,745	23,772	8,189	23,235
8	PNBK	18,259	96,928	10,188	16,963	11,927	54,465	11,346	70,395
9	PD	128,659	427,522	101,260	78,902	73,824	358,718	39,422	238,452
10	PKPI	56,902	89,040	36,624	24,371	15,580	64,962	23,348	59,494
11	PPDI	32,627	53,508	6,816	19,146	5,518	36,170	9,782	33,278
12	PPNUI	60,890	38,416	9,328	22,724	8,210	32,840	6,513	68,068
13	PAN	280,249	317,697	284,432	164,523	224,825	234,608	67,777	215,717
14	PKPB	37,548	89,507	43,867	27,580	57,573	61,854	37,115	158,246
15	PKB	80,781	125,270	30,738	66,468	64,503	143,501	28,384	266,405
16	PKS	192,469	427,724	236,858	135,903	68,846	204,870	61,906	290,796
17	PBR	156,192	229,335	81,967	118,805	45,219	182,154	23,995	121,427
18	PDIP	86,312	825,584	75,839	211,513	142,588	576,596	63,499	676,798
19	PDS	7,014	339,483	10,136	61,623	16,292	31,364	7,943	32,468
20	GOLKAR	340,971	1,133,411	577,323	619,056	316,039	714,399	178,513	772,890
21	PANCASILA	30,404	171,126	13,876	30,182	11,000	29,452	9,972	28,497
22	PSI	30,860	52,748	15,778	26,365	9,025	28,969	10,757	24,713
23	PPD	21,305	50,055	32,527	24,245	12,993	24,562	19,707	15,912
24	PP	11,451	119,432	7,097	16,552	7,502	45,547	12,878	59,260
	TOTAL	2,105,477	5,538,736	2,010,545	2,066,708	1,278,080	3,369,800	752,696	3,574,522

No.	Party	Bangka Belitung	Riau Archipelago	Jakarta	West Java	Central Java	Yogyakarta	East Jakarta	Banten
1	PNI	2,495	9,257	9,480	81,868	143,387	15,130	127,196	27,781
2	PBSD	2,542	8,557	11,845	60,695	50,105	7,011	82,326	24,382
3	PBB	102,492	17,550	68,831	606,841	209,639	34,942	270,281	150,921
4	MERDEKA	1,218	3,573	7,417	101,776	74,972	12,817	114,481	42,308
5	PPP	35,953	34,092	386,614	2,189,484	1,593,219	94,268	1,407,803	454,033
6	PPDK	4,432	10,796	29,621	93,994	55,507	10,015	79,013	38,936
7	PPIB	11,523	12,462	9,783	38,926	53,373	3,011	44,760	29,290
8	PNBK	8,751	7,110	16,084	116,759	167,194	13,453	182,865	33,459
9	PD	25,014	36,802	958,763	1,634,523	1,179,898	108,544	1,568,587	382,652
10	PKPI	3,397	4,746	17,702	185,202	134,022	10,072	184,939	40,823
11	PPDI	4,645	4,344	16,063	94,417	138,937	10,571	115,987	34,243
12	PPNUI	2,482	4,713	23,212	134,612	60,591	13,122	172,063	90,439
13	PAN	23,299	64,941	333,116	1,119,011	1,352,029	342,921	1,001,002	237,585
14	PKPB	4,279	9,298	86,603	440,592	285,547	67,415	407,739	124,379
15	PKB	16,970	21,777	164,249	1,062,963	2,578,241	193,476	6,297,366	189,838
16	PKS	26,619	61,565	1,057,246	2,369,231	839,356	141,114	608,810	520,202
17	PBR	12,299	13,965	137,678	391,219	176,593	14,001	219,529	182,073
18	PDIP	91,785	81,447	664,245	3,625,476	5,245,879	503,321	4,325,918	615,098
19	PDS	3,973	38,509	253,205	233,664	206,781	32,038	237,330	78,574
20	GOLKAR	87,698	90,034	433,966	5,775,780	2,803,991	266,444	2,691,619	943,050
21	PANCASILA	1,828	18,010	25,557	128,208	58,379	7,384	211,790	42,833
22	PSI	2,303	4,719	9,651	76,401	46,527	6,665	79,157	35,528
23	PPD	1,379	3,464	5,637	48,123	54,933	12,474	50,245	49,698
24	PP	1,372	4,395	10,084	92,690	122,706	4,438	77,992	13,663
	TOTAL	478,748	566,126	4,736,652	20,702,455	17,631,806	1,924,647	20,558,798	4,381,788

continued on next page

APPENDIX 3.1 – cont'd

No.	Party	Bali	West Nusa Tenggara	East Nusa Tenggara	West Kalimantan	Central Kalimantan	South Kalimantan	East Kalimantan	North Sulawesi
1	PNI	65,294	17,776	29,515	14,812	7,600	3,396	6,919	6,911
2	PBSD	5,475	8,514	25,775	18,455	6,054	9,819	16,831	3,206
3	PBB	4,155	233,282	24,243	38,554	26,145	79,043	44,708	14,847
4	MERDEKA	7,799	38,427	33,496	18,783	8,586	10,157	11,803	5,945
5	PPP	17,226	174,386	36,330	157,351	70,627	220,735	108,250	37,814
6	PPDK	7,264	37,838	54,004	49,287	11,862	11,890	38,873	5,486
7	PPIB	44,537	21,212	20,470	21,451	5,167	10,622	5,200	5,372
8	PNBK	48,868	23,814	33,820	72,639	9,880	18,514	14,743	14,494
9	PD	121,665	89,468	83,281	114,950	66,430	74,500	75,281	172,321
10	PKPI	43,102	33,528	78,719	31,982	16,238	20,048	14,321	26,347
11	PPDI	19,741	25,801	71,540	28,364	9,135	11,243	6,575	3,800
12	PPNUI	866	29,864	14	13,149	6,190	32,116	8,472	2,414
13	PAN	20,456	124,357	29,398	79,455	49,402	125,239	77,251	18,709
14	PKPB	79,924	40,912	34,374	44,518	12,915	34,433	17,372	23,207
15	PKB	27,050	84,350	54,031	52,662	37,902	115,799	48,812	26,562
16	PKS	18,837	111,471	19,827	66,608	25,137	166,847	129,819	18,939
17	PBR	2,260	159,457	6,829	68,943	33,694	100,364	31,091	16,055
18	PDIP	999,889	139,158	396,619	330,226	190,630	137,989	187,000	195,090
19	PDS	13,181	6,705	120,340	77,436	33,645	11,318	51,176	178,021
20	GOLKAR	320,710	491,394	758,869	459,252	223,498	323,298	368,782	388,469
21	PANCASILA	4,249	25,537	33,229	14,358	4,006	13,988	45,557	11,019
22	PSI	3,715	37,295	22,237	25,453	6,382	7,482	6,308	6,031
23	PPD	4,651	28,918	31,018	50,163	6,238	9,598	9,270	11,432
24	PP	23,686	27,053	51,917	28,558	6,800	8,761	22,285	9,447
	TOTAL	1,904,600	2,010,517	2,049,895	1,877,409	874,163	1,557,199	1,346,699	1,201,938

Source: Compiled from <www.kpu.go.id>.

APPENDIX 3.2

Votes Composition of the 2004 Parliamentary Election Results for DPR-RI by Party and Province

No.	Party	N. Aceh Darussalam	North Sumatra	West Sumatra	Riau	Jambi	South Sumatra	Bengkulu	Lampung
1	PNI	0.60	1.18	0.48	0.88	1.34	1.55	1.51	1.80
2	PBSD	0.64	2.01	0.61	1.45	0.91	0.70	1.41	0.71
3	PBB	5.31	2.43	5.80	4.03	3.34	4.10	3.96	1.94
4	MERDEKA	1.62	0.95	1.51	0.86	1.14	1.19	0.97	0.49
5	PPP	13.84	7.18	11.68	8.12	5.82	6.47	8.27	4.79
6	PPDK	2.32	1.29	0.92	2.70	1.29	1.46	1.36	1.98
7	PPIB	0.97	2.15	0.68	1.39	0.76	0.71	1.09	0.65
8	PNBK	0.87	1.75	0.51	0.82	0.93	1.62	1.51	1.97
9	PD	6.11	7.72	5.04	3.82	5.78	10.65	5.24	6.67
10	PKPI	2.70	1.61	1.82	1.18	1.22	1.93	3.10	1.66
11	PPDI	1.55	0.97	0.34	0.93	0.43	1.07	1.30	0.93
12	PNUI	2.89	0.69	0.46	1.10	0.64	0.97	0.87	1.90
13	PAN	13.31	5.74	14.15	7.96	17.59	6.96	9.00	6.03
14	PKPB	1.78	1.62	2.18	1.33	4.50	1.84	4.93	4.43
15	PKB	3.84	2.26	1.53	3.22	5.05	4.26	3.77	7.45
16	PKS	9.14	7.72	11.78	6.58	5.39	6.08	8.22	8.14
17	PBR	7.42	4.14	4.08	5.75	3.54	5.41	3.19	3.40
18	PDIP	4.10	14.91	3.77	10.23	11.16	17.11	8.44	18.93
19	PDS	0.33	6.13	0.50	2.98	1.27	0.93	1.06	0.91
20	GOLKAR	16.19	20.46	28.71	29.95	24.73	21.20	23.72	21.62
21	PANCASILA	1.44	3.09	0.69	1.46	0.86	0.87	1.32	0.80
22	PSI	1.47	0.95	0.78	1.28	0.71	0.86	1.43	0.69
23	PPD	1.01	0.90	1.62	1.17	1.02	0.73	2.62	0.45
24	PP	0.54	2.16	0.35	0.80	0.59	1.35	1.71	1.66
	TOTAL	100.00	100.00	100.00	100.00	100.00	100.00	100.00	100.00

continued on next page

APPENDIX 3.2 – cont'd

No.	Party	Bangka Belitung	Riau Archipelago	Jakarta	West Java	Central Java	Yogyakarta	East Jakarta	Banten
1	PNI	0.52	1.64	0.20	0.40	0.81	0.79	0.62	0.63
2	PBSD	0.53	1.51	0.25	0.29	0.28	0.36	0.40	0.56
3	PBB	21.41	3.10	1.45	2.93	1.19	1.82	1.31	3.44
4	MERDEKA	0.25	0.63	0.16	0.49	0.43	0.67	0.56	0.97
5	PPP	7.51	6.02	8.16	10.58	9.04	4.90	6.85	10.36
6	PPDK	0.93	1.91	0.63	0.45	0.31	0.52	0.38	0.89
7	PPIB	2.41	2.20	0.21	0.19	0.30	0.16	0.22	0.67
8	PNBK	1.83	1.26	0.34	0.56	0.95	0.70	0.89	0.76
9	PD	5.22	6.50	20.24	7.90	6.69	5.64	7.63	8.73
10	PKPI	0.71	0.84	0.37	0.89	0.76	0.52	0.90	0.93
11	PPDI	0.97	0.77	0.34	0.46	0.79	0.55	0.56	0.78
12	PPNUI	0.52	0.83	0.49	0.65	0.34	0.68	0.84	2.06
13	PAN	4.87	11.47	7.03	5.41	7.67	17.82	4.87	5.42
14	PKPB	0.89	1.64	1.83	2.13	1.62	3.50	1.98	2.84
15	PKB	3.54	3.85	3.47	5.13	14.62	10.05	30.63	4.33
16	PKS	5.56	10.87	22.32	11.44	4.76	7.33	2.96	11.87
17	PBR	2.57	2.47	2.91	1.89	1.00	0.73	1.07	4.16
18	PDIP	19.17	14.39	14.02	17.51	29.75	26.15	21.04	14.04
19	PDS	0.83	6.80	5.35	1.13	1.17	1.66	1.15	1.79
20	GOLKAR	18.32	15.90	9.16	27.90	15.90	13.84	13.09	21.52
21	PANCASILA	0.38	3.18	0.54	0.62	0.33	0.38	1.03	0.98
22	PSI	0.48	0.83	0.20	0.37	0.26	0.35	0.39	0.81
23	PPD	0.29	0.61	0.12	0.23	0.31	0.65	0.24	1.13
24	PP	0.29	0.78	0.21	0.45	0.70	0.23	0.38	0.31
	TOTAL	100.00	100.00	100.00	100.00	100.00	100.00	100.00	100.00

No.	Party	Bali	West Nusa Tenggara	East Nusa Tenggara	West Kalimantan	Central Kalimantan	South Kalimantan	East Kalimantan	North Sulawesi
1	PNI	3.43	0.88	1.44	0.79	0.87	0.22	0.51	0.57
2	PBSD	0.29	0.42	1.26	0.98	0.69	0.63	1.25	0.27
3	PBB	0.22	11.60	1.18	2.05	2.99	5.08	3.32	1.24
4	MERDEKA	0.41	1.91	1.63	1.00	0.98	0.65	0.88	0.49
5	PPP	0.90	8.67	1.77	8.38	8.08	14.18	8.04	3.15
6	PPDK	0.38	1.88	2.63	2.63	1.36	0.76	2.89	0.46
7	PPIB	2.34	1.06	1.00	1.14	0.59	0.68	0.39	0.45
8	PNBK	2.57	1.18	1.65	3.87	1.13	1.19	1.09	1.21
9	PD	6.39	4.45	4.06	6.12	7.60	4.78	5.59	14.34
10	PKPI	2.26	1.67	3.84	1.70	1.86	1.29	1.06	2.19
11	PPDI	1.04	1.28	3.49	1.51	1.04	0.72	0.49	0.32
12	PPNUI	0.05	1.49	0.00	0.70	0.71	2.06	0.63	0.20
13	PAN	1.07	6.19	1.43	4.23	5.65	8.04	5.74	1.56
14	PKPB	4.20	2.03	1.68	2.37	1.48	2.21	1.29	1.93
15	PKB	1.42	4.20	2.64	2.81	4.34	7.44	3.62	2.21
16	PKS	0.99	5.54	0.97	3.55	2.88	10.71	9.64	1.58
17	PBR	0.12	7.93	0.33	3.67	3.85	6.45	2.31	1.34
18	PDIP	52.50	6.92	19.35	17.59	21.81	8.86	13.89	16.23
19	PDS	0.69	0.33	5.87	4.12	3.85	0.73	3.80	14.81
20	GOLKAR	16.84	24.44	37.02	24.46	25.57	20.76	27.38	32.32
21	PANCASILA	0.22	1.27	1.62	0.76	0.46	0.90	3.38	0.92
22	PSI	0.20	1.85	1.08	1.36	0.73	0.48	0.47	0.50
23	PPD	0.24	1.44	1.51	2.67	0.71	0.62	0.69	0.95
24	PP	1.24	1.35	2.53	1.52	0.78	0.56	1.65	0.79
	TOTAL	100.00	100.00	100.00	100.00	100.00	100.00	100.00	100.00

continued on next page

APPENDIX 3.2 – cont'd

No.	Party	Central Sulawesi	South Sulawesi	Southeast Sulawesi	Gorontalo	Maluku	North Maluku	West Irian Jaya	Papua	National
1	PNI	0.65	0.31	0.80	0.27	1.27	0.57	2.75	5.93	0.81
2	PBSD	0.45	0.44	0.51	0.16	0.66	0.22	4.37	1.06	0.56
3	PBB	4.86	2.73	6.23	5.38	4.57	4.40	3.70	1.04	2.62
4	MERDEKA	1.24	1.91	0.93	0.22	1.19	0.32	1.71	1.91	0.74
5	PPP	7.00	6.56	11.33	13.01	5.80	6.75	5.81	1.55	8.15
6	PPDK	1.68	6.65	1.26	0.97	0.88	9.63	10.46	4.88	1.16
7	PPIB	0.81	0.66	0.78	0.22	1.10	0.21	0.76	3.64	0.59
8	PNBK	0.41	0.63	7.13	0.01	2.27	1.69	2.37	3.61	1.08
9	PD	5.33	3.04	2.05	0.89	4.02	6.44	3.76	4.57	7.45
10	PKPI	4.55	1.85	1.54	0.12	2.30	2.27	2.47	3.67	1.26
11	PPDI	0.52	0.38	0.63	1.45	1.06	1.37	2.10	1.12	0.75
12	PPNUI	0.62	0.69	0.52	0.09	1.43	0.54	0.00	0.19	0.79
13	PAN	4.67	6.40	7.27	4.37	5.28	5.90	2.64	4.62	6.44
14	PKPB	2.37	1.67	1.51	1.04	2.09	1.59	1.78	3.44	2.11
15	PKB	2.51	1.74	2.21	3.45	2.16	1.27	2.32	5.14	10.57
16	PKS	3.82	7.30	4.40	3.37	7.29	10.57	2.85	2.31	7.34
17	PBR	2.39	2.93	3.25	3.30	3.87	2.67	1.51	0.56	2.44
18	PDIP	6.92	4.55	7.72	6.09	18.48	9.09	13.06	8.08	18.53
19	PDS	6.30	1.87	0.68	0.72	8.57	8.27	8.21	6.34	2.13
20	GOLKAR	38.59	44.34	36.81	53.07	20.74	23.53	24.83	24.70	21.58
21	PANCASILA	2.18	0.55	0.64	1.20	1.05	0.09	0.48	3.73	0.95
22	PSI	0.75	1.34	0.47	0.30	1.02	1.67	2.06	1.55	0.60
23	PPD	0.50	0.72	0.43	0.28	1.49	0.64	0.00	2.76	0.58
24	PP	0.89	0.73	0.91	0.00	1.42	0.30	0.00	3.60	0.77
	TOTAL	100.00	100.00	100.00	100.00	100.00	100.00	100.00	100.00	100.00

Source: Calculated from Appendix 3.1.

Selected References

Ali, Muhammad. "Critical Assessment of Muslim Political Pluralism in Indonesia". *Jakarta Post* daily, 21 July 2004.

Ananta, Aris, Evi Nurvidya Arifin, and Leo Suryadinata. *Indonesian Electoral Behaviour. A Statistical Perspective*. Singapore: Institute of Southeast Asian Studies, 2004.

Doni, Anton. "Nostalgia the Only Thing PBB Has to Offer Voters". *Jakarta Post*, 21 January 2004.

Hari, Kurniawan. "Agung Elected House Speaker". *Jakarta Post*, 2 October 2004.

IFES. "Results from Wave I and II Tracking Surveys", 10 February 2004a.

———. "Results From Wave I through IX of Tracking Surveys", no date, 2004b.

———. "Results From Wave X of Tracking Survey", 28 April 2004c.

———. "Results From Wave XI through XII of Tracking Surveys", 1 June 2004d.

———. "Results From Wave XIII of Tracking Survey", 23 June 2004e.

———. "Results From Wave XIV of Tracking Survey", 1 July 2004f.

———. "Results from Wave XV of Tracking Survey", 4 August 2004g.

———. "Report on Tracking Survey Wave 16", no date, September 2004h.

———. "Results from Wave XVII of Tracking Survey", 15 September 2004i.

———. "Results from Wave XVIII of Tracking Survey", 19 October 2004j.

Jakarta Post. "Golkar Back in Power at House". 7 May 2004a.

———. "Akbar Wants Golkar to Get House Speakership". 1 October 2004b.

———. "Cabinet People". 23 October 2004c.

Komisi Pemilihan Umum. *Buku Lampiran IV Pemilihan Umum 1999*.

Hasil Pemilihan Umum Anggota Dewan Perwakilan Rakyat 1999. Jakarta: Komisi Pemilihan Umum, 1999.

Kompas. "Konvensi Golkar Sisakan Akbar dan Wiranto". 20 April 2004*a*.

—. "Ungguli Akbar Tanjung Wiranto Capres Tunggal Partai Golkar". 21 April 2004*b*.

—. "Baru 10 Partai Politik Tanda Tangani Hasil Pemilu". 6 May 2004*c*.

—. "Capres-cawapres Sudah Berjanji, Rakyat Menunggu Bukti", 5 July 2004*d*.

—. "Kalla: Jumlah Anggota Kabinet 34 Orang", 11 October 2004*e*.

—. "Yudhoyono Panggil Calon Menteri Mulai 15 Oktober". 13 October 2004*f*.

Kuntowijoyo. "Menuju Pragmatisme Religius" [Toward Religious Pragmatism] *Kompas* daily, 7 July 2004.

LSI. "Final LSI National Survey Predicts: Victory for SBY in the Presidential Election. Analysis of LSI Survey Findings 16 September 2004". Jakarta: Lembaga Survey Indonesia, no date.

—. "Voter View on the First 100 Days of the SBY-Kalla Government. Analysis of LSI Survey Findings. Analysis of LSI Survey Findings. October 2004". Jakarta: Lembaga Survey Indonesia, 2004*a*.

—. "The Contrasting Public Image of President SBY. Analysis of LSI Survey Findings 7–8 December 2004". Jakarta: Lembaga Survey Indonesia, 2004*b*.

Lubis, Satria Hadi. *Yang Nyata dari PK Sejahtera.* Fourth edition. Jakarta: Misykat Publication, 2004.

NDI. "The People's Voice: Presidential Politics and Voter Perspectives in Indonesia". Report based on a series of focus group discussions conducted during May in seven Indonesian provinces ahead of the July 2004 presidential elections. Jakarta (?): National Democratic Institute for International Affairs (NDI), 2004.

Piliang, Indra J. "PKS Support for Amien and the Wiranto Factor". *Jakarta Post*, 7 July 2004.

Pikiran Rakyat. "Capres Konvensi Masih 6 Orang". 18 April 2004.

Sari P. Setiogi. "PDS to Lead by Moral Example for New Nation". *Jakarta Post*, 16 January 2004.

Sherlock, Stephen. "The 2004 Indonesian Elections: How the System Works and What the Parties Stand For". A report on political parties. Canberra: Centre for Democractic Institution, Australian National University, February 2004.

Suryadinata, Leo, Evi Nurvidya Arifin, and Aris Ananta. *Indonesia's*

Population. Ethnicity and Religion in a Changing Political Landscape.
Singapore: Institute of Southeast Asian Studies, 2003.

Suryadinata, Leo. *Elections and Politics in Indonesia.* Singapore: ISEAS,
2002.

——. *Military Ascendancy and Political Culture: A Study of Indonesian
Golkar.* Athens, Ohio: Centre of International Studies, 1989.

Taufiqurrahman, M. "Fuming Akbar Send PPP Packing". *Jakarta Post,*
3 October 2004.

The Parliament of the Commonwealth of Australia. "The Parliamentary
Elections in Indonesia — 5 April 2004. Report of the Australian
Parliamentary Observer Delegation". Canberra: Commonwealth of
Australia, May 2004.

Tirtosudarmo, Riwanto. "Cross-Border Migration in Indonesia and the
Nunukan Tragedy". In *International Migration in Southeast Asia,* edited
by Aris Ananta and Evi Nurvidya Arifin. Singapore: Institute of
Southeast Asian Studies, 2004.

Tempo. "Jangan Percaya Hasil Polling". *Tempo, edisi pemilihan presiden
2004,* 30 June 2004, p. 131.

TEMPO Interaktif "Sulawesi Selatan Didesak Dipecah Menjadi Enam
Provinsi". 28 April 2001. <http://www.tempointeraktif.com>.

Valentino, Hank. "Who will be the Winners in the 2004 Elections?".
Political Outlook, *Jakarta Post* <http://www.thejakartapost.com/
outlook/po107.asp>.

Wiratma, I Made Leo. "Perkembangan Politik Triwulan Kedua (April-
Juni) 2004: Dari Pemilu Legislatif menuju Pemilu Presiden". *Analisis
CSIS: Mencermati Hasil Pemilu 2004.* vol. 33, no. 2. Jakarta: Centre
for Strategic and International Issues, 2004.

Index